Anglo-Saxon England

DAVID BROWN

Drawings by
PIPPA BRAND

ROWMAN AND LITTLEFIELD
TOTOWA, NEW JERSEY

FRONTISPIECE
The uncovering of the Sutton Hoo sword, viewed by the
owner of the site, Mrs E. M. Pretty, seated between friends
on the edge of the trench. In the burial chamber W. F.
Grimes and Stuart Piggott are watched by T. D. Kendrick
and Sir John Forsdyke of the British Museum.

First published in the United States 1978
by Rowman and Littlefield, Totowa, N.J.

ISBN 0-8476-6045-1

PRINTED IN GREAT BRITAIN

CONTENTS

ACKNOWLEDGMENTS

Of the many friends who have helped in the preparation of this book I should like especially to thank David Miles who has allowed me to quote so extensively from his unpublished excavations at Berinsfield; Simon Mitchell who read Chapter 5 and made suggestions for its improvement; and David Hinton who, perhaps unwittingly, provided the idea for Chapter 10.

Author and publisher join in thanking those who have gone to considerable trouble to provide photographs. We thank especially Peter Addyman, Nigel Kerr, Stanley West, Tim Champion, David Kelly, Leslie Alcock, Angela Evans, Rosemary Cramp, Suzanne Keene, Jim Gould, Andrew Oddy, Calvin Wells, Tom Hassall and Mary Craster.

Thanks are due to the following for permission to reproduce black-and-white photographs: the Trustees of the British Museum, frontispiece and pages 49, 51, 53, 55, 59, 82, 83, 98; York Archaeological Trust, pages 8, 91, 92; the Master and Fellows of Corpus Christi College, Cambridge, pages 11 and 76; Merseyside County Museums, Liverpool, page 18; Nigel Kerr, page 20; Norwich Castle Museum and Mary Kippen, pages 21, 97, 99; Oxfordshire Archaeological Unit, pages 23 (John Cowan, photographer), 105, 107; Ashmolean Museum, Oxford, pages 25, 26, 29, 31, 38, 74, 75, 100; West Stow Environmental Archaeological Group, page 34; Ipswich Museum, page 37; Camelot Research Committee, pages 43, 44, 45, 46; A. F. Kersting, page 65; Rosemary Cramp, pages 66 and 67; Winchester Research Unit, pages 69, 71, 87; T. Haigh, page 77; Cambridge University, Museum of Archaeology and Ethnology, page 94; Worthing Museum, page 95 (*top*); *Antiquities Journal*, page 95 (*bottom*); Brian Hope Taylor, page 103.

Thanks for permission to use coloured photographic material are due to: Oxfordshire Archaeological Unit, jacket photograph; Ashmolean Museum, facing page 16; Maidstone Museum, facing page 17 (*top*); Merseyside County Museums, Liverpool, facing page 17 (*bottom*); Southampton University, Department of Archaeology, facing page 32 (*top*); Camelot Research Committee, facing page 32 (*bottom*); British Library, facing page 33; the Trustees of the British Museum, facing pages 80 (*top* and *bottom*), 81 (*top*) and 96 (*top*); the Dean and Chapter, Winchester Cathedral, facing page 81 (*bottom*); Jim Gould, facing page 96 (*bottom*); the town of Bayeux, with special permission, facing page 97.

The drawing on page 33 is based on one by R. Warmington in *Medieval Archaeology* 16, 1972; the plan on page 35 is based on one by Stanley West which appeared in *Medieval Archaeology* 13, 1969; the drawing on page 41 is after one by Leslie Alcock in *The Quest for Arthur's Britain*, edited by G. Ashe, Pall Mall Press 1968; the drawings on pages 70 and 85 are after two by Martin and Birthe Kjølbe Biddle; the drawing on page 88 is based on one by Jim Gould in *Transactions of the South Staffordshire Archaeological Society* 9, 1968; the drawing on page 89 is based on one by Philip Rahtz in *The Archaeology of Anglo-Saxon England*, edited by D. M. Wilson, Methuen 1976; the drawing on page 90 is after one by Peter Addyman which appeared in *Antiquities Journal* 54, 1974.

The quotation on pages 52 and 53 is printed with the permission of O. G. S. Crawford and thanks are also due to Macmillan, London and Basingstoke, for permission to quote from *Beowulf* in Kevin Crossley-Holland's translation on page 54.

INTRODUCTION

The story of Anglo-Saxon England spreads over more than six hundred years. It begins with the collapse of Roman Britain, and the arrival of Anglo-Saxon settlers from across the North Sea early in the fifth century; and it comes to an end with the Norman Conquest of 1066.

The early settlers were from the first their own masters in a new country. They had not been subjected to Roman rule in their homelands, and by the time they came to Britain the Roman way of life was disintegrating; they were free to follow their own traditional ways. The stone buildings of the Roman towns and villas were unfamiliar to them; they built their houses of timber, choosing to settle on new sites, many of which have remained the sites of villages ever since. They spoke their own language which has become the English which is spoken and written today. They brought with them also their beliefs in their own gods but, in the seventh century, these gave way to Christianity following the mission of Augustine from Rome. In the wake of Christianity there was increased contact with France and Italy, bringing men with education and learning and craftsmen with skills which had been unknown in England since Roman times. In this subtly different way the Anglo-Saxons came under the influence of the Roman culture.

The term Anglo-Saxon is a modern one. It is a convenient one to use when referring to this period of English history, but it implies a degree of unity which was never there. There were never any such people as the 'Anglo-Saxons'. The first settlers were predominantly 'Angles' and 'Saxons' but there were others—'Jutes' and 'Frisians' for example—who made up the medley of people who came to England. The early settlers kept to their tribal groups, forming kingdoms and sub-kingdoms, the small ones subservient to the large ones and eventually being taken over by them. By the ninth century the country was divided between the four kingdoms of Northumbria, Mercia, East Anglia and Wessex. The first three of these fell to the

Vikings and when they were eventually reconquered it was by Alfred's successors, the kings of Wessex. With the death in 954 of Eric Bloodaxe, the Viking ruler of York, England was permanently united under a single king.

Archaeologists have found the Anglo-Saxons most elusive. Graves and grave goods there have been in plenty, but other traces of Anglo-Saxon life have seemed negligible to those who dug in the hope of finding remains as substantial as those of a Roman building. Many must have dug away the Anglo-Saxon deposits without recognising them, and then declared that there was nothing to be found. We now know that this could not be further from the truth, although it is really only in our own lifetime that excavators have been able to recognise and have paid particular attention to looking for the evidence of this period. Now they have found it, in quantity and often in the most unexpected form, and each year brings a fresh crop of discoveries to add to the growing picture of life in Anglo-Saxon England.

Excavations in the Coppergate, York, in 1977 uncovered the remains of timber houses and workshops of the tenth century. Earlier buildings (in lower levels) have yet to be excavated.

1

Anglo-Saxon Origins

The key to the history of England in Anglo-Saxon times is the *Anglo-Saxon Chronicle*. This is a year-by-year account of all the major happenings, the rise and fall of kings and bishops, the important battles, and other major events, running from Roman times right through to the Norman Conquest and beyond.

The *Chronicle* begins its account of the coming of the Saxons with the story of Hengist and Horsa in AD 449. The entry for that year reads:

> 'Hengist and Horsa were invited by Vortigern, king of the Britons, and they came to Britain at a place called Ebbsfleet; first they came to help the Britons, but afterwards they fought against them.'

The subsequent entries describe how Horsa was killed, but Hengist won several battles and eventually the kingdom. Ebbsfleet is near Sandwich in eastern Kent, and the kingdom referred to is obviously that of Kent. After this episode, the entries in the *Chronicle* go on to describe the arrival and success of Aelle in Sussex and then of Cerdic in Wessex; but that is all. Nothing is said about the arrival of the Anglo-Saxons anywhere else in England. By the time the *Chronicle* takes up the story in other parts of the country, it is clear that the newcomers had already been settled there for some time. Thus the account of the earliest years of the Anglo-Saxon settlement in England which is given by the *Chronicle* is incomplete—and it is not difficult to see why this is so.

The *Chronicle* was compiled from information collected from many different sources. It was first put together in its present form in the time of Alfred at the end of the ninth century, and the compilers

OPPOSITE
A page from the *Anglo-Saxon Chronicle* covering the years 418–454. Entries are written opposite the years in which they occur; the entry for 449 towards the bottom of the page mentions Hengist and Horsa in the second line. At the time of the compilation of the *Chronicle* only a few events were known for these early years; hence many of the years are without entries and the page has blanks.

working at that time made use of whatever written evidence they could find, though this did not always cover the earliest periods. The Anglo-Saxons did not learn to read and write till after the spread of Christianity which followed the coming of Augustine in AD 597. It was not till after that, and in most parts of the country not till well on in the seventh century, that events of any sort could be recorded in writing. By then the coming of the Anglo-Saxons was more than two hundred years away and it is not surprising that there was no clear recollection of their arrival in many parts of the country. Perhaps we should even wonder whether the accounts which we have for Kent and Sussex and Wessex are totally reliable; it is probably best to regard them as traditional rather than completely accurate accounts of the settlement of those areas.

We get a far better picture of the newcomers from the writings of the monk the Venerable Bede who lived and worked at the monastery at Jarrow on the south bank of the River Tyne between about AD 672 and 735. Bede's most famous book is his *Ecclesiastical History of the English Church and People* written in 731. In it he says little about the first coming of the Saxons. He has the basic story of Hengist and Horsa, but from there he jumps straight to church affairs and the arrival of Augustine. But Bede does tell us something about who the newcomers were:

'They came from three of the stronger peoples of Germany, the Saxons, the Angles and the Jutes. From the Jutes came the Cantuarii [the people of Kent] and the Victuarii who are the people who occupy the Isle of Wight and those who live opposite the Isle of Wight, on the mainland, in the territory of the West Saxons and are to this day called the nation of Jutes. From the Saxons, that is the region which is now called Old Saxony, came the East Saxons, the South Saxons and the West Saxons. From the Angles, that is the country which is called Angeln and which from then till now has remained deserted, and which lies between the lands of the Saxons and the Jutes, came the East Angles, the Middle Angles, the Mercians, and all of the Northumbrian race, that is the people who live north of the Humber, as well as the other Anglian tribes.'

In this paragraph Bede tells us not only who the newcomers were and where they came from, but also where they settled in England. This is far more than we learn from the uncertain entries at the beginning of the *Chronicle*. Indeed it is only when provided with all this information that we realise just how little the *Chronicle* reveals.

an. cccc.xuiii	Her romane gesomnodon
an. cccc.xix.	alra þold hord feondra þe
an. cccc.xc.	ene þafon þ sume on uþ
an. cccc.xci.	þan ahreddon þ hie na
an. cccc.xcii.	nig mon siþþan findan ne
an. cccc.xciii.	meahte þ sume mid him
an. cccc.xciiii.	on gallia leddon : ·
an. cccc.xcu	
an. cccc.xcui	
an. cccc.xcuii.	
an. cccc.xcuiii.	
an. cccc.xcix.	
an. cccc.xx.	Her palladius se biþe
an. cccc.xxi.	þ scrobniende to scottú
an. cccc.xxii.	þ hehtiud geleapan
an. cccc.xxiii.	tirmede epo celestino
an. cccc.xxiiii.	þam papun : ·
an. cccc.xxui	
an. cccc.xxuii	
an. cccc.xxuiii	
an. cccc.xxuiiii	
an. cccc.xxxix.	
an. cccc.xl.	
an. cccc.xli.	
an. cccc.xlii.	
an. cccc.xliii.	Her þendon þ hist palas to rome þ heo fultomes bedon þiþ hia þan
an. cccc.xliiii.	uiþ þan manne þon þe hi fyrdedon þið ætla huna ǫ niþes þa þendan hi
an. cccc.xlui.	to anglú þngsel cynni æðelingas ðer þleau bardan
an. cccc.xluii	
an. cccc.xluiii.	
an. cccc.xlix.	Her mauri þ qualentinus on fenzon rice þucrodon.uii. þintr
an. cccc.l.	þon þissú dagú hengest þ horsa þno fritt gupine geleaþade
an. cccc.li.	bretta to kninge þ geohton bretre onþam staþe þe is gnemned
an. cccc.lii.	ypping fleot ahere bretú to fultume achie þet onhie fuhton
an. cccc.liii.	

In giving this information Bede seems to have anticipated just the sort of questions we might ask; perhaps they are the questions he asked himself, for he inserted this passage right in the middle of his version of the Hengist and Horsa story. It reads very much as though he said to himself as he copied the story down from his own sourcebooks, 'That doesn't tell anybody very much. It doesn't even say who they were or where they came from. I know more about that myself.' And he proceeded to add in these details which are of great interest and importance to us today.

There has never been any reason to doubt Bede's information, for it is possible to identify the places he was talking about with fair certainty; virtually the same names are used today. In north-west Germany, bordering on the North Sea, there is the region of Lower Saxony. In northern Denmark there is the province of Jutland, the land of the Jutes. And, between the two, as Bede says, there is an area called Angeln which now forms a small part of the province of Schleswig-Holstein at the neck of the Danish peninsula.

The areas which Bede talks about in Denmark and north Germany had been the homes of farming people for many hundreds of years before the migrations to England. The people there lived well outside the frontiers of the Roman Empire so, unlike the inhabitants of Britain, they had never been subjected to Roman rule. Nevertheless, they must have known something about the Romans, for traders from the south brought Roman goods to exchange for their products, and they would have heard of the Roman way of life, the walled towns full of stone buildings, the country villas and the mile upon mile of metalled roads. Theirs was a simpler life which has left only their deserted village sites and their graveyards. It is the material from these sites by which our ancestors are best known before they came to England.

In the areas of the Angles and the Jutes, in Denmark, the most abundant sort of evidence is the pottery from the burials. Most of the dead were cremated and their ashes were placed in pots which were buried in the ground. Hundreds of these cremation pots have been found, and they have provided archaeologists with a vast amount of material to study. All the various differences of shape and styles of decoration have been used to divide the pottery up into a number of regional types. Inevitably the pottery from the region which corresponds best to the area of Angeln has been labelled 'Anglian', though it would be naïve to suppose that the Angles thought of themselves as the people who used a particular type of pottery. So far

Typical cremation pots from the cemetery at Süderbrarup in Angeln.

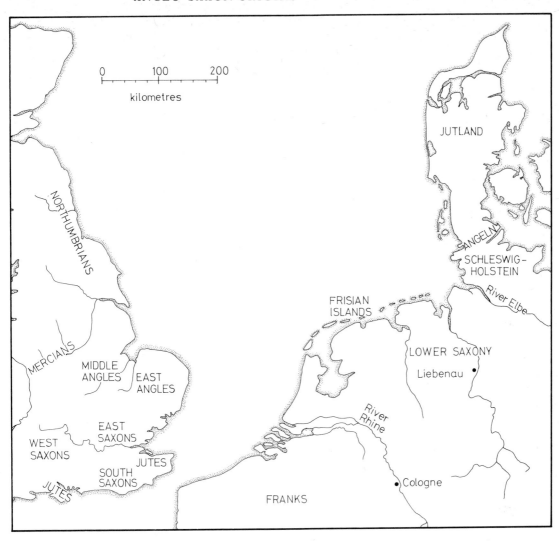

as can be seen, there is no reason to suppose that the people who used the pottery which has been labelled Anglian were in any way different from their neighbours whose pottery was slightly different. The customs of all these cremating people appear to be much the same, and it will need some details more definite than a variation in pottery styles to distinguish between two different peoples such as the Angles and the Jutes.

Further south, in that part of north Germany from which the Saxons are said to have come, there do appear to be some differences. In this area some of the dead were cremated, but others were buried in ordinary graves, so-called 'inhumations'. This changing custom was due to the influence of the Roman world to the south where

13

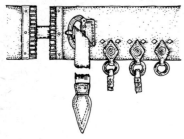

A Roman military belt with bronze fittings, from the grave of a Germanic warrior found at Liebenau, Lower Saxony.

inhumation burial had been the normal fashion since the second century. Amongst these inhumation burials there are a fair number of graves of men who were buried with weapons and military equipment—swords, spears, shields and military belts. This equipment was not locally made, but was the standard Roman military equipment of its day, and it is certain that these men must once have been soldiers in the Roman army. No doubt, as young adventurers, they had gone south from their homeland to the Roman frontier on the River Rhine where they had signed on as mercenaries in the Roman army. Some of these men stayed and settled in the lands where they served, for their graves are found in various parts of northern France as well as along the frontiers of the Empire; but others returned to their homes in the north after their campaigns and they took their kit with them. Doubtless they had many stories to tell, and were looked on as heroes who were admired for the deeds which they had done. And when they died it was appropriate that they should be buried with their uniforms and their weapons. Graves with this sort of equipment in them are found in Holland and Germany as far north as the great cemeteries along the banks of the River Elbe.

These warrior graves in north Germany provide a simple explanation of Vortigern's actions. He had first invited Hengist and Horsa to fight for him, so the story goes. It is hardly likely that he would have sought the help of untried men, and what now seems likely is that Hengist and Horsa and their followers were former Roman mercenaries who had served their time in the Roman army and had gone back home afterwards. These were men whom the Roman army had trained and equipped, men who had actually fought for the Empire. From Vortigern's point of view, they were the next best thing to the Roman army itself, and *that* he could not get. So Vortigern recruited his own mercenaries; and when they arrived they quickly discovered that Roman Britain had had its day. All Hengist and Horsa had to do was to turn against Vortigern and take his kingdom from him; and as soon as the word got back home, others followed them.

This sort of explanation of the situation puts the *Chronicle*'s story in a much more plausible light. But it does not explain the sort of state that Britain itself was in, nor why Vortigern needed help.

The Roman armies had finally been withdrawn from Britain early in the fifth century. They were required nearer home to defend the centre of the Empire and could not be wasted in garrisoning the far-flung province of Britain that was of little value. So Britain was abandoned, and the local officials who remained were left to act as best they could. There were raids from Scotland and from Ireland and there was civil unrest too, and it was to try to cope with these troubles that Vortigern had sought help from outside. This is the gist of the historical story—but we know from the evidence of archaeological finds that there was more to it than that.

Archaeology has shown that there was a complete breakdown in the normal way of life at the end of the fourth century or the beginning of the fifth. This is seen most dramatically in the lack of new building and the lack of any new manufactured objects. In particular Roman pottery, the commonest find in any Roman excavation, just disappears. In the latter part of the fourth century there had been a flourishing pottery industry; workshops in many parts of the country were making a wide range of good quality vessels and supplying them to a wide market. Then suddenly the industry collapsed. So far as it is possible to tell from the archaeological finds, no single workshop outlasted any other for any considerable period of time. It was as though the whole industry closed down within a period of a very few years, and things must have been in a poor state for this to have happened. A measure of the chaos which brought about the collapse can be seen from the fact that not one of those potters who must have been put out of work subsequently tried to restart business on a smaller scale somewhere else when the situation improved again. Of course, the pottery industry was only one of the many activities that were affected, but its sudden collapse and disappearance provides perhaps the most dramatic illustration of the chaos into which Roman Britain was plunged.

When exactly did all this happen, and when did Hengist and Horsa come? Was it in AD 449 as the *Chronicle* suggests, or was it at some other date? Archaeology cannot answer this question in precise terms, but it can give some clues. On the Continent, in northern France and Belgium, where soldiers and their families from north Germany had settled before the end of Roman rule, there was no unrest. The new settlers rapidly switched from using their own handmade products to the superior Roman products, and when eventually they took control of the country, their demand for the better products kept the Roman industries going; glass factories, potteries, bronze-casting workshops, all continued to flourish.

Why, we should ask, didn't the same thing happen in England? The answer can only be that the Roman industries had already collapsed and ceased production *before* the Anglo-Saxon settlers

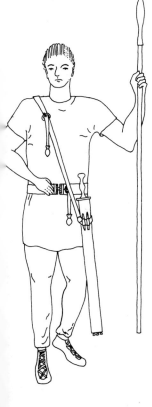

Reconstruction drawing of the warrior from Liebenau, wearing his Roman equipment.

OPPOSITE
The brooches, beads
and buckle discovered
in a rich woman's
grave at Berinsfield,
Oxfordshire, displayed
as they would have
been worn by their
sixth-century Saxon
owner. (*See page 22*)

arrived in any number. We know that the pottery industry in Britain kept going up to about AD 400, but we cannot trace it any further. The collapse, when it came, appears to have happened overnight, though it is probably realistic to think in terms of a gradual but rapid decline lasting some ten or twenty years. This suggests that we should not expect to find the Anglo-Saxons coming as settlers before about AD 420; but thereafter, at whatever date they did come, they would have found Britain a ruined country, and far from having to invade and conquer, their arrival can have been little more than a walk-over.

2

Pagan Cemeteries

The antiquaries of the eighteenth and nineteenth centuries were enthusiastic explorers of the cemeteries of their early ancestors, and. they speculated at length about the origins of the objects which they found. The graves of the Anglo-Saxons were first recognised as a result of the work of two clergymen, the Reverend Bryan Faussett and the Reverend James Douglas, who excavated widely in Kent between 1757 and 1792. Both men were unusually careful in recording their findings. Douglas published his in a book, *Nenia Britannica*, which he illustrated himself; Faussett recorded his in a series of notebooks which are now kept with his collection in the Merseyside County Museums, Liverpool. Although they were both digging the same sort of graves and finding the same sort of objects, they did not agree on the date of the finds. Faussett thought that the graves and the objects in them had belonged to the Romans, for he could not believe that the splendid objects which he found had been made by the Anglo-Saxons. But Douglas showed that they had; he pointed to the evidence of the excavations, and his reasoning was quite clear:

> 'The Roman claim to these sepulchres must be totally out of the question. A very brief remark will suffice for proof. The coins of Anthemius [Emperor in Italy, AD 467–472], Clovis [King of the Franks, AD 481–511] and Justinian [Byzantine Emperor, AD 527–565] found in the barrows, will without further discussion prove them to have existed *after* the departure of the Romans.'

No more convincing argument could be brought forward even today.

Throughout the nineteenth century many new Anglo-Saxon

Above
The gold, silver and garnet jewellery of a wealthy Jutish woman buried at Bifrons, near Canterbury in the sixth century. (*See page 27*)

Below
This exotic jewelled brooch, found at Kingston in Kent, represents the changing fashions of the seventh century.

17

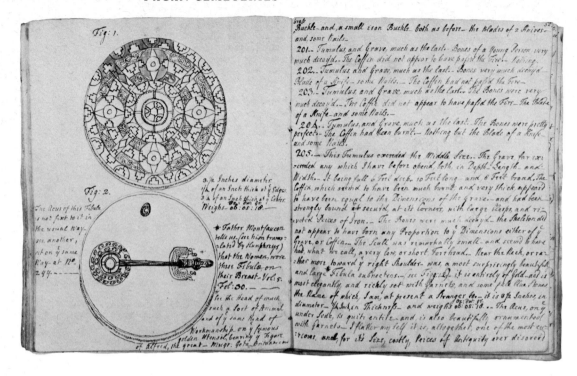

Faussett's notebook with entries describing the graves he excavated at Kingston, Kent, with his own drawing of the jewelled brooch from grave 205—the finest example of this seventh-century type. (*See opposite page 17*)

cemeteries were found, though not all of them were as well recorded as these early excavations. The publications of the archaeological societies are littered with accounts of new finds and illustrations of new pieces. A great deal of new information was recorded, but discussion was limited mainly to the identification of the objects and comparisons with similar pieces. There was little attempt to try to read further into the facts which had been unearthed. It remained for E. T. Leeds to show how this could be done.

E. T. Leeds first became interested in the Anglo-Saxons when he joined the staff of the Ashmolean Museum in Oxford in 1908. Five years later he wrote a little book entitled *The Archaeology of the Anglo-Saxon Settlements*. In it he attempted to use the mass of information from the graves to retell the history of the early days of settlement in England. Leeds considered the distribution of the various cemeteries around the country, and their dates, and the dates of the various different classes of objects found in the graves, and this gave him information which allowed him to fill in the scanty story told in the *Chronicle*.

But Leeds found that the story which he put together from the archaeological evidence was not the same as the story recorded in the *Chronicle*; and at times the two stories, far from supporting each

18

other, were actually contradictory. This brought Leeds, and archaeology, into conflict with what was then the traditional historical approach—of relying on the written evidence alone.

The most striking example of disagreement between Leeds's archaeological approach and the conventional historical approach concerned the conquest of Wessex. This episode is described as fully as any series of events in the early years of the *Chronicle*. It began with the arrival of Cerdic and Cynric on the south coast in AD 495. The years following were ones of consolidation of the coastal areas and of the capture of the Isle of Wight. Then in 552 Cynric moved north to Salisbury; in 556 Cynric and Ceawlin fought the British at Barbury in Wiltshire; in 577 Ceawlin took Cirencester, Gloucester and Bath, and by 584 he had moved into Oxfordshire. The conquest had proceeded steadily from the south coast northwards.

Leeds showed that the archaeological evidence contradicted this story. The objects from the cemeteries in the Thames Valley, particularly those around Abingdon and Dorchester-on-Thames, indicated that Anglo-Saxon settlers were already living there

A comparison of the advance of the West Saxons from the south coast, as recorded in the *Chronicle*, with the distribution of the 'early' cemeteries in the Thames Valley.

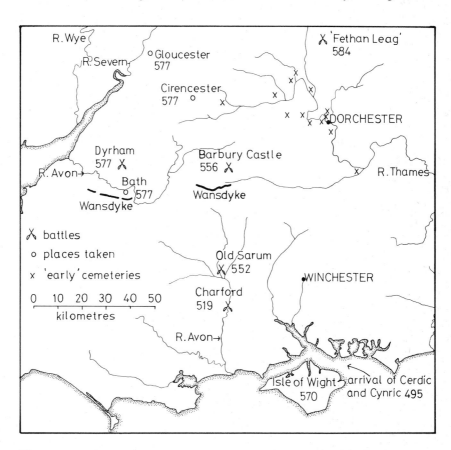

Cremation pots in the course of excavation at Loveden Hill, Lincolnshire.

peacefully in the fifth century, a hundred years before the *Chronicle* says that they arrived; but the cemeteries on the south coast were generally later than the date when Cerdic and Cynric are said to have arrived. And the dates weren't the only thing wrong, for the number of cemeteries known in the two areas suggested that there were far more settlers in the Thames Valley than there had ever been on the south coast.

Leeds did not dismiss the evidence of the *Chronicle*, but he was forced to conclude 'that the historical accounts only represent one side of the story, and that they do no more than record the doings of one section of the tribe which ultimately constituted the population of Wessex'. The major part of the tribe, so the archaeological evidence suggested, had settled in the Thames Valley in the fifth century, having arrived there by coming up the river. Leeds's verdict is accepted by most archaeologists today, though it is ironical to record that he himself subsequently changed his mind about the river route and suggested that the first settlers in the Upper Thames Valley had come overland from the Wash. Nevertheless, Leeds's method remains firmly established, and gone for ever are the days of relying solely on the written historical sources.

A prime example of Leeds's method is the way in which our knowledge of Anglo-Saxon settlement in the northern and eastern areas of England has been built up from the evidence of the pottery used as containers for cremated bones, for in these parts of England cremation seems to have been the burial practice which was preferred by the new arrivals.

There are few objects in the cremation cemeteries, but there is no shortage of pots. Some of the cemeteries are enormous: at Loveden Hill in Lincolnshire over 1,200 pots have been excavated, and at Spong Hill near North Elmham in Norfolk over 1,000 pots have been excavated in a cemetery which may contain as many as 5,000. Many of the pots found in cremation cemeteries like these are similar to those which were being used on the Continent; it is possible to trace the same pottery traditions in England and on the Continent, and in some cases perhaps even the work of the same potters. There can be no doubt that the people buried in these vast cemeteries had come across from Denmark and north Germany; but the question of when they came remains difficult to answer—for pots by themselves are notoriously difficult to date.

Archaeologists are divided on this question. Some argue that there are pots which are so similar to pots dated to the fourth century on the Continent that the people who used them must have come here in the fourth century when Britain was still under Roman rule. Others say that this dating is too early, and that none of the cemeteries can have been used before the Romans departed at the beginning of the fifth century; this, after all, is the date of the earliest of the few metal objects to have been found in the cremation pots. But, irrespective of which date may eventually be shown to be the correct one, these vast cremation cemeteries do provide evidence of Anglo-Saxon settlements which are not even hinted at in the *Chronicle* until the middle of the sixth century.

Cremation pots from the cemetery at Caistor-by-Norwich.

In other parts of the country cemeteries are a mixture of cremations in pots and ordinary inhumed burials, or all the graves are inhumed ones. These inhumations contain a great variety of objects in striking contrast to the sameness of the pottery from the cremations. Men were buried with their weapons and women with their beads and jewellery, and both often have a drinking vessel of some sort, a pot, a small bucket or a glass.

A cemetery excavated at Petersfinger, near Salisbury, in 1948 contained a number of well-equipped graves of men and women. One of these, grave 60, was the grave of an elderly man. By his side lay his

OPPOSITE
The richest lady from
Berinsfield, with her
beads and brooches
lying as they were
worn at the burial.

spear, the point by his head, the butt by his feet. The wooden shaft
had rotted away and was not even visible as a stain in the chalky soil,
but the distance between the point and the butt showed that the spear
had been a full two metres long. Overlying his chest was the iron boss
which had covered the centre of his shield, and above and below it
were two pairs of rivets which had been fitted to the shield board. The
board, which was made of wood and leather, had also rotted away
completely, but the position of the rivets shows that the shield must
have been at least forty-five centimetres in diameter, and it could not
have been much bigger or it would not have fitted into the grave. At
the man's waist there was an iron belt buckle, and by his shoulder a
small wooden bucket—a drinking vessel—held together with a
bronze binding. This man is typical of very many found in Anglo-
Saxon cemeteries; his grave can be matched by examples from all over
the country.

These numerous finds show that the spear and the shield were the
normal weapons of an ordinary man. Swords, though not rare, are far
less common, being found with only about one in ten of the armed
men; and there are also other adult men who have no weapons at all. It
seems probable that these three types, the swordsman, the spearman
and the unarmed man, represent three distinct social classes amongst
the Anglo-Saxons. Spearmen—the most common—should be
thought of as ordinary freemen, and swordsmen as members of the
aristocracy, while the unarmed men were perhaps serfs—the slaves of
Anglo-Saxon society. It appears that when it came to burial, the rule
was 'as in life, so in death' and the men were buried with the weapons
appropriate to their class. This is probably the most realistic way of
thinking of all these weapons in the graves. The impression of
constant warfare which they tend to give is a most misleading one.

In women's graves it is the position of the objects which gives the
best clues to their function in life and, nowadays, every care is taken to
make as accurate a record as possible during excavation. A good
example is provided by one of the graves recently excavated by David
Miles, the assistant director of the Oxford Archaeological Unit, in a
cemetery at Berinsfield, near Dorchester-on-Thames.

The cemetery was discovered when the ground was being cleared to
dig gravel, and the excavation had to be carried out quickly to avoid
delay to the quarrying. Nevertheless each grave was uncovered and
carefully cleared by hand, and the bones of each skeleton and the
objects around it were recorded in drawings and photographs as the
work proceeded. One of the most notable graves was number 102, the

Petersfinger, grave 60:
plan of the skeleton
and grave goods as
excavated.

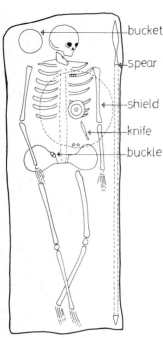

bucket

spear

shield

knife

buckle

grave of a woman laid out in the usual fashion. At her waist was a large buckle, the only part of her belt to have survived, and nearby was an iron knife which must have been tucked into her belt. Over her chest and her neck were a mass of beads and a number of brooches. The first to be uncovered, on her left shoulder, was a large brooch which was rectangular at one end and trefoil-shaped at the other—a type of brooch known to archaeologists as a 'great square-headed brooch'. Beneath this brooch was another, a dish-shaped brooch—a type known as a 'saucer brooch'. On the right shoulder was a second saucer brooch, a pair to the first. Scattered about around and between the brooches were a number of beads with many more clustered between the chest and the right arm.

Excavating all these objects was a task requiring great patience for, when first uncovered, the beads, most of which were of amber, looked exactly like the small gravel pebbles which covered them. The job was well done and the main cluster of beads was revealed as four lines between the right arm and the body with a further two lines extending erratically across the chest to the left shoulder. Once cleared it became easy to see that they represented a long double string most of which lay in the four lines of the main cluster, but which originally hung in two strands between the two saucer brooches. There was no sign that the beads ever went round the neck. After the long strings of amber had been removed, more tiny glass beads were discovered in the disturbed area between the two saucer brooches. These did not form a regular line, for many of them had fallen down among the rib bones, but from their position it was reasonable to reconstruct them as a short string stretching across between the two brooches. Thus the lady appears to have been wearing three strands of beads, a short strand of glass beads and two long strands of amber beads, well over a hundred beads in all.

The brooches were more than just decoration for they served as the necessary and functional fastenings of the dress and they provide a clue to the sort of dress which was being worn. In places on the surfaces of the brooches tiny scraps of cloth were preserved by the corrosion of the bronze. On the backs of the saucer brooches there were fragments of the woollen braid which had formed the edge of the garment and through which the pins had been fastened. On the back of the great square-headed brooch there were numerous traces of a very fine linen cloth, and this same cloth was also found on the *fronts* of the saucer brooches. There is thus evidence for two different garments, a linen garment covering the fronts of the saucer brooches

Petersfinger, grave 60: reconstruction of the man with his weapons.

24

Fragments of linen preserved by the corrosion on the back of the great square-headed brooch from Berinsfield, grave 102.

and fastened somewhere in the middle by the big brooch, and a woollen garment underneath this fastened by the two saucer brooches on the shoulders with the beads hanging in strings between them. The underneath garment must have been some sort of dress, the over garment a sort of cloak.

This collection of objects shows that this Berinsfield lady was a rich one, on a par with the aristocratic swordsmen of her day. While most

25

Typical Saxon gilt bronze saucer brooch, from Fairford, Gloucestershire.

Typical Anglian cruciform brooch, from Ixworth, Suffolk.

cemeteries contain a few graves as rich as this, the average ordinary woman was buried with only two brooches and perhaps a few beads. The two brooches, whatever their shape, correspond to the pair of saucer brooches in the Berinsfield grave and served as shoulder fastenings for the dress. In the Saxon areas of England the main type of brooch was the saucer brooch; sometimes they were cast solid in bronze, sometimes they were made up of several thin sheets of bronze soldered together; usually they were gilded and decorated with a geometric or spiral or animal pattern. In the Anglian areas of England the women favoured a long plain bronze brooch which archaeologists have named the 'cruciform brooch'. The name is derived from the way the knobs stick out from the headplate like the arms of a cross. These cruciform brooches have as many different varieties as the saucer brooches, and both vary somewhat during the two hundred years during which they were so popular. The cruciform brooches are more obviously functional than the saucer brooches for they are shaped like a vast safety-pin, the spring being hidden under the head at one end, and the point fastened in a catch-plate under the foot at the other. The distinctive feature of the cruciform brooch is the way in which the foot is shaped into the head of an animal. In its earliest and simplest forms the animal looks a bit like a horse, but the later examples have been elaborated so much that the animal is no longer recognisable. The positions in which the brooches are found in the graves shows that they were worn with the head of the animal at the top though archaeologists, perversely, normally refer to this part as the foot of the brooch; the result is that illustrations in books and museum displays nearly always show the brooches upside down! There are other types of brooch besides the cruciform and saucer types and they too have their areas of popularity, but none is as diagnostic of the two main areas of Anglo-Saxon England as are the cruciforms and the saucers.

A difference in brooches, by itself, does not distinguish one group of people from another any more than pottery styles can, but between the Anglian and Saxon areas of England the differences go further than just a difference in types of brooch. In many Anglian women's graves, in addition to the pair of cruciform brooches, there is found by each wrist a pair of small bronze clasps. These clasps come in all sorts of shapes and sizes but they all work in the same way, like a hook and eye. These clasps were sewn to the cuff and served to fasten the two edges together like cufflinks. The significance of these wrist-clasps is that they indicate that Anglian ladies liked their sleeves closed at the wrist, but since there is no such evidence for Saxon ladies we may assume that their sleeves were open and perhaps wider too. Thus without even any surviving piece of cloth it is possible to say that there was not only a difference between the sorts of brooch which were favoured in the two areas, there was also a difference in the styles of dress.

The whole question of Anglian dress fashions has recently been the subject of a study by a German scholar, Hayo Vierck. He has compared the sorts of fashions found in England with those found in Denmark and southern Norway and Sweden, and he has shown that all belonged to the same tradition. That is to say that although we may think of the Angles as coming solely from Angeln as Bede says, archaeologically they are really indistinguishable from the people who were living in the rest of southern Scandinavia. Cruciform brooches and wrist clasps were the fashion there too, and the cultural group to which our Anglians belonged is more widespread than Bede implies.

Bede's third group of people, the Jutes, are also recognisable by the objects which they used. The cemeteries in the Jutish areas, eastern Kent and the Isle of Wight, show an interesting mixture of influences which set these areas apart from the Anglian and Saxon areas. A good example of these influences is given by the contents of a woman's grave from the cemetery at Bifrons, just east of Canterbury. The grave, number 29, was a large one and the lady was buried in it with all her jewellery and personal ornaments. By her neck was found a pair of round silver brooches, with gilded surfaces set with red garnet; between the brooches there was a necklace of amber and glass beads, and hanging from the necklace were four thin sheet gold pendants known as 'bracteates'. At her waist was a pair of silver-gilt 'radiate head brooches', and below them a collection of iron keys and rings. She also wore a plain bronze armlet and finger rings, and she had a belt buckle. Around her skull were some fragmentary gold threads which were originally woven into a headband.

The most distinctive of the objects in this grave are the thin gold pendants, the 'bracteates'. These certainly come from Scandinavia, and quite probably from Denmark. They are a particularly Scandinavian type of ornament, based originally on Roman medallions, but by this time adapted to show figures of Scandinavian mythology. These pieces are certain evidence of a continuing contact between the Jutes of Kent and their former homeland. In England such bracteates are found only in Kent.

The pair of 'radiate head brooches' are Frankish; they come from

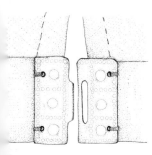

How wrist clasps were used to fasten sleeves.

An iron seax, from Chadlington, Oxfordshire. The handle, fitted over the tang at the lower end, made a weapon about 50 cms long.

northern France or perhaps the Rhineland, where they are very common. These pieces must have been made there and brought across to Kent where they serve as evidence of the particularly close contacts which developed between Kent and the Continent in the sixth century.

Finally there is the pair of round silver brooches set with garnets. These are a local type, made in Kent, and as characteristic of the Kentish cemeteries as the saucer and cruciform brooches are of the cemeteries in other areas.

These objects from Bifrons are typical of the world of the Jutes; similar sorts of objects are found throughout eastern Kent and to a lesser extent in the Isle of Wight in the sixth century. They differ from the objects in Anglian and Saxon graves in two respects. Firstly they show evidence of widespread contacts abroad, particularly with the kingdom of the Franks across the Channel; secondly they show that the Jutes were a wealthy people. The Berinsfield grave may have been a rich one, but here is richness of quite a different order. At Berinsfield there was bronze and gilt bronze, but here at Bifrons there are gold and silver and polished garnets. These are the distinctive features of the kingdom of Kent at this time.

The graves which have been described all belong to the sixth century. This is the period when Bede's subdivision of the English tribes is best illustrated by finds from the graves, and when the distribution maps of the various different types of objects show the most distinct differences between the various peoples. Earlier than this, in the years when the Anglo-Saxon settlements were beginning, there appears to have been a good deal of movement about the country and the patterns of distribution are less distinct. Later, in the seventh century, there was a definite change of fashion throughout the country and the differences between the tribal areas disappeared, at least as far as the objects in graves are concerned.

For women there was quite literally a fashion change. The pairs of brooches which are so characteristic a feature of the graves of the sixth century appear no more; though very occasionally a single elaborate brooch is worn in the centre of the chest. This seems to imply that the cumbersome garments fastened with two brooches were replaced by a type of dress which didn't really require any fastening at all; perhaps it had an open neck like a shirt or a blouse which might occasionally have been fastened with a brooch. In men's graves there is a marked decrease in the quantities of weapons buried, and in many seventh-century cemeteries weapons are extremely rare. Where they occur

28

Gold cross studded with garnets, from a woman's grave at Stanton, Ixworth, Suffolk.

they often take the form of a long one-edged knife, the seax, rather than the familiar spear and shield-boss. The cemeteries too seem to be more regularly laid out with the graves all orientated west to east, with the heads of the skeletons at the west as today, whereas before it was common to find several distinctly different orientations in the same cemetery.

These changes of fashion are often attributed to the coming of Christianity. Certainly there are quite distinctly Christian objects — crosses, for example — in some graves. However, the fashion changes which we have noticed seem to have been too widespread too early for them all to be attributed solely to Christianity. Augustine came to Kent in AD 597, but it was not till the 630s and the 650s that some other parts of England became even nominally Christian, and conversion cannot have happened overnight; it must have taken many years to spread throughout the population.

It seems, then, more likely that the change in the burial customs during the seventh century is due as much to the spread of new ideas and fashions which were becoming popular on the Continent at the same time as to anything else. Kent, with its widespread Continental contacts, was the first to be affected by these new influences, and from Kent they spread gradually throughout the country. As far as England was concerned, Christianity, which had been established on the Continent since the end of the fifth century, was but a part of this new influence.

It was not till the eighth century that the church established full control over the burial of the dead. Churchyards came into use then and the old pagan cemeteries were gradually abandoned.

3

Saxon Villages

In May 1921 E. T. Leeds received a letter from a friend who was on holiday at Sutton Courtenay, just south of Abingdon. In the course of his holiday rambles the friend had come across a gravel pit in which workmen had dug up a number of baked clay rings, like large doughnuts; he thought Leeds would be interested, so he sent him one. Leeds recognised the baked clay ring as a type of object of which he already had several in his care at the Ashmolean Museum in Oxford. They were thought to belong to the pre-Roman Iron Age, but no one was sure, and this seemed a good opportunity of finding out; so Leeds visited the site. He learned that the quarrymen had discovered the clay rings and also a quantity of pottery in a hollowed-out pit in the top of the gravel. This hollow was roughly rectangular, about two and a half by four metres and two-thirds of a metre deep; it had been filled up with dark soil which the quarrymen had shovelled away so that they could get to the gravel below.

As the quarrying proceeded, the men came across more of these rectangular hollows, and Leeds visited the site from time to time to explore them. They were remarkably similar, sometimes oval, sometimes rectangular, always dug down into the top of the gravel. At each end, at the bottom of the hollow, there was a hole twenty-five or thirty centimetres in diameter, filled with dark soil—the setting for a stout vertical post.

The filling of the hollows was mainly dark soil amongst which were pieces of handmade pottery, bone objects such as combs and pins, and loose stones, as well as more baked clay rings. Leeds no doubt recognised the handmade pottery and the bone objects as Saxon, but if he had any doubts these were quickly dispersed by the magnificent

The gilt bronze equal-armed brooch found in hut 10 at Sutton Courtenay.

silver gilt brooch which he found wedged down behind one of the post holes in his tenth hollow. This sort of brooch is a rare but most distinctive type characteristic of the earliest phases of Anglo-Saxon settlement in England. The clay rings were thus identified as Anglo-Saxon too, though it was many years before it was discovered that they are actually loomweights used to hold taut the warp threads of a vertical loom.

Leeds explained the rectangular hollows with their two post holes as the remains of Anglo-Saxon huts. He suggested that the holes had contained posts, and that these had been like tent poles supporting a ridge pole from which a thatched roof had sloped down on each side almost to ground level. The floor of the hut would have been the gravel bottom of the hollow, and the walls the sides of the hollow perhaps raised above ground level with low turf walls. There wouldn't have been much room inside, but it would have been possible to stand in the centre and to sit or squat on benches or logs around the sides.

In the following years Leeds continued to explore the hut-hollows as they were exposed in the gravel quarry, but the picture did not change, and by 1947 his plan showed an area of some twenty acres dotted with more than thirty of these small huts. In the meantime other hut-hollows had been found elsewhere. Mostly these were accidental finds, but all conformed to the Sutton Courtenay pattern of shallow hollows with a substantial post hole at each end.

Leeds would have been the first to admit that the huts which he had discovered were not very grand, yet he never seems to have had any doubts about them. In 1936 he wrote:

'In such cabins, with bare headroom, amid a filthy litter of broken bones, of food and shattered pottery, with logs or planks raised on stones for their seats or couches lived the Anglo-Saxons.'

But this was plainly more than some writers were prepared to believe. In a survey written in 1948, the Council for British Archaeology declared:

'It is impossible to imagine a man of the type buried in the Taplow barrow having no more adequate domestic amenities in life than those provided by a wattled hut of the Sutton Courtenay model.'

Other writers echoed the same view. Quite clearly it was difficult to accept that conditions were that awful despite the lack of any evidence for anything better.

31

A nineteenth-century sunken hut from Athelney, Somerset. This is the sort of building which Leeds imagined that his Sutton Courtenay huts looked like.

OPPOSITE
Above
Postholes of houses and fences from a seventh- and eighth-century Saxon village at Chalton in Hampshire have been revealed by carefully removing the soil and cleaning the chalk below.

Below
An aerial view of the hilltop earthworks of Cadbury Castle, Somerset, originally constructed in the Iron Age and refortified during the Age of Arthur.

A way out of this difficulty was proposed by Dr C. A. Ralegh Radford in 1957. He had taken note of the finds from excavations on the Continent in Germany and Holland, and he was able to point out that hut-hollows, or sunken huts, of the Sutton Courtenay type were found there too. He noticed, however, that they were never the only type of hut found on a site, but were just one of several different varieties. Always round about the sunken huts there were larger buildings without hollows erected from large timbers set into post holes. Radford pointed to two places at Sutton Courtenay where Leeds had found rows of post holes, and he suggested that there may have been larger post-built houses there too in between the sunken huts. If this was so it is easy to see why Leeds didn't find them, for his method in this case had been to recognise the huts by their hollows showing in the face of the gravel quarry. Obviously he wouldn't have found any huts or houses that didn't have hollows!

Dr Radford's comments were a warning that if we were ever to understand what an early Saxon village was like, then we must make sure that we excavated all of it. This meant that excavations would have to uncover a large area and explore the entire surface of the old site, so that post holes, rubbish pits, working areas and pathways could all be identified along with the sunken hollows. This has now become the normal method of excavating Anglo-Saxon village sites.

In recent years sunken huts have been discovered in many places, but often these have not been suitable for widespread excavation because the sites are in built-up areas, in or near towns and villages. This is hardly surprising, for if we consider that most of our modern villages date back to Saxon times then it is to be expected that there will be traces of Anglo-Saxon huts beneath them. It will only be on those sites which for some reason were abandoned during Saxon times that we are likely to find the whole area of an old settlement

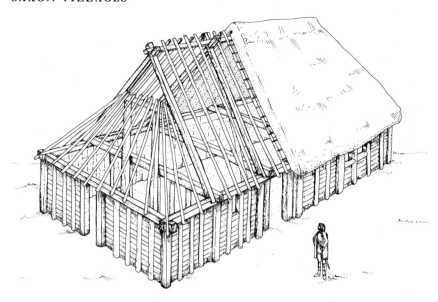

A possible reconstruction of one of the houses at Chalton.

A decorative page from the Lindisfarne Gospels, which incorporates designs derived from both British and Anglo-Saxon metalworking traditions.

undisturbed by later buildings. Sometimes these sites are found by chance, as the Sutton Courtenay site was, though more often nowadays a deliberate search on the ground and from the air will suggest that a site is there. From the air little is to be seen of the post hole buildings, but sunken huts create a distinctive rectangular crop mark which we have now learned to recognise; a search of the ground, if ploughed, is likely to produce pottery and perhaps other objects.

One site which has been extensively excavated is at West Stow in Suffolk. The finds from the excavation show that the site was occupied in the fifth and sixth centuries, but was abandoned in the seventh century. The site became farmland again, only to be covered later in the Middle Ages by a thick layer of windblown sand. This has protected the remains of the Saxon village from being disturbed by modern deep ploughing.

The excavations at West Stow are rescue excavations, carried out on behalf of the Department of the Environment by Mr Stanley West. He has been able to show that the site was covered with sunken huts and also with the regularly arranged post holes of more substantial buildings of just the type which Radford had predicted. These rectangular buildings seem to form a focus around which the sunken huts are grouped, as though the rectangular building was the main house of the group and the sunken huts were the working sheds surrounding it. The advantages in opening up large areas all at once were evident in the number of other interesting features which were discovered. There were several extensive areas where the subsoil

Reconstructed huts at West Stow.

appeared to have been worn away into shallow hollows; the pieces of bone and pottery in the soil filling these hollows are all very worn. Stanley West has suggested that this may be due to trampling by animals and that the hollows may represent the positions of temporary enclosures for livestock. Not all the features are explicable, though. For example, a series of neatly dug rectangular pits in the centre of the site seem not to have been for rubbish, for the soil filling them is 'clean'; they are, perhaps, for 'retting' flax.

An even more remarkable village is in course of being excavated at Chalton in Hampshire. The site of the village is the windblown crest of the chalk downland. The ground has a very poor covering of soil and is only able to produce a crop with the extensive use of fertilisers. For many years the farmer, Mr J. Budden, has been collecting and recording all finds and traces of ancient settlement on his farm. In only one place was there any suggestion of early Saxon settlement, and this was up on the down. Trial excavation showed that this site was indeed the remains of a village, and now it is being excavated, a little at a time each year, by the staff and students of the Department of Archaeology at Southampton University. Each year a new part of the village is explored by removing the thin covering of soil and cleaning the surface of the chalk by scraping it or brushing it, and so revealing the plans of a complex series of buildings. In contrast to West Stow, the Chalton houses are nearly all the post type; only two sunken huts have been discovered so far.

There seem to have been two methods of building a house with posts. The most popular way was to set the posts in individual holes about a metre apart and build up a framework for the building in this way; but a few of the houses are indicated by shallow trenches outlining the walls. Either the posts were set up individually in the trenches, or perhaps a wooden sill beam sat in the trench and the posts

34

were set into this. The houses are all rectangular and vary between about three by five and a half metres and four and a half by ten metres. Most of them had two doors opposite each other in the middle of the long sides—an arrangement which is known elsewhere and which seems to have been familiar to Bede who quotes a story in which he compares the brief life of a man on earth to the 'flight of a sparrow through the hall, coming in at one door and immediately out at the other'. Another feature of many of the Chalton houses is an internal partition which separates off an area about a fifth of the whole at one end. This reflects something of the domestic arrangements of the

Plan of part of the excavations at West Stow.

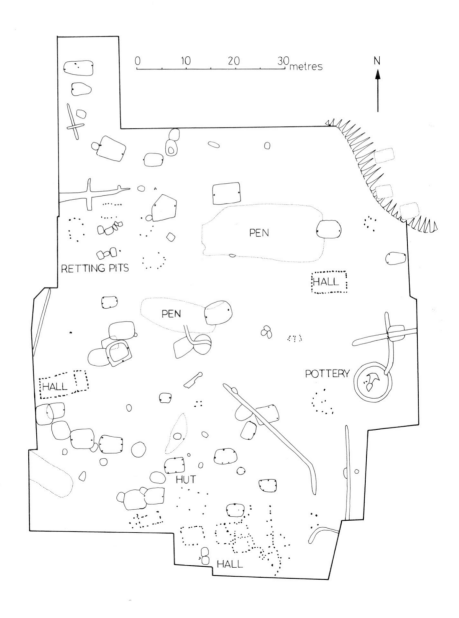

houses, but all trace of floors and hearths has gone, so thin is the covering of the surface soil.

The excavations at Chalton continue; the limits of the settlement have not yet been reached in any direction and it is impossible to predict how large the village may turn out to be. But already the plan is showing some interesting features. Some of the houses overlap one another, and clearly the buildings belong to different phases; there appear to have been several phases of rebuilding of entire houses. There are also some interesting groups of houses, in threes, one on each of three sides of an open square. One of these groups of three houses is enclosed by its own fence which was made, so the line of semi-circular post holes shows, of split logs. As the excavations at Chalton continue, so our picture of what an Anglo-Saxon village was like begins to take shape.

The results from Chalton conform more closely to what we may expect of the dwellings of the Anglo-Saxon settlers; they approximate to what we may call a village. The dates of the West Stow settlement are known from the finds to belong to the earliest phase of settlement. Chalton looks as though it is going to be later, probably from the seventh and eighth centuries, though at the moment there is an amazing lack of finds from the site. A measure of the difference between the two sites is the presence of many of the sunken huts at West Stow and their almost complete absence at Chalton. It seems probable that this type of hut went out of fashion during the seventh century, and was replaced by rectangular buildings of a more conventional sort.

Despite the rectangular buildings which have been found on the earliest sites as Radford predicted, the sunken hut remains the commonest type of dwelling on these early sites. But not all archaeologists agree on Leeds's reconstruction and there is considerable argument as to what the huts were really like. Some favour Leeds's view, that a ridge pole between the uprights supported a pitched roof sloping down to low walls of turf or wattles, and that the natural gravel at the bottom of the hollow was the floor. Others maintain that it would have been impossible to live and work in such conditions and that there must in practice have been a wooden floor over the hollow. This latter view seems to be supported by the fact that there are no trampled floor layers at the bottoms of the hollows, and there is no sign of burning due to hearths placed on the gravel. Yet, if there was a floor over the hollow, why dig a hollow in the first place? There seem to be good arguments for both views.

A double line of loomweights lying where they fell from the loom in a hut at Pakenham, Suffolk.

Stanley West's excavations have come nearer to solving this dilemma than any others. He is fortunate that comparatively little erosion has taken place on his site. One of his sunken huts was full of ring-shaped loomweights like those which had first attracted Leeds to Sutton Courtenay. Underneath the loomweights he found quite definite traces of timber, and also more remains of charred timber on top of them. His comment on this was, 'Having seen huts burned down in Africa, I noticed that they always burn upwards; the roof catches the main fire first and then that falls in on the furniture inside, and the walls are either left standing charred or they fall in on top.' This seems to be what happened to two of the huts at West Stow.

A second decisive piece of evidence comes from the fireplaces. Stanley West found hearths, built on pads of clay, situated not in the bottom of the hollows, but on the edges of the hollows, so that during collapse after abandonment of the hut, part of the hearth on its clay pad slipped down into the hollow, but part remained on the edge of the hollow.

Both these pieces of evidence indicate that the sunken huts must have had floors across the hollows. The loomweights would have been resting on the 'floor' of the hut or suspended a very little above it, and the wood found underneath them can only be the planking of the

37

floor. The clay pad and the hearth must once have been in one piece and on the level of the floor of the hut. Here we have no sign of timber, but the position of the piece of the hearth surviving on the lip of the hollow shows what the original level of the hearth and the floor must have been. The hearth in this position also shows that the walls of the hut cannot be where we have imagined them right on the edge of the hollow. If there was to be room for the hearth without damaging the walls, then they must have been set back about a metre from the edge or perhaps ever further.

The outcome of Stanley West's finds has been the creation of a West Stow Environmental Archaeology Group which has made replicas of the sort of huts which he discovered. Members have built a hut with a hollow in the middle between the two major posts, but floored with a wooden floor which extends about a metre out from the edges of the hollow; the walls are of split oak timbers and do not require large posts for their support. The hut is no longer a squalid hovel, but a reasonable rectangular hut some five metres by six and with sufficient headroom for a man to stand up anywhere inside.

Stanley West has succeeded in bringing the earliest Anglo-Saxons out of their sunken huts and putting them into serviceable dwellings. We still have to find out what the hollows were for; but whatever their purpose, they made it possible for Leeds to recognise the site of an Anglo-Saxon village in the first place.

E. T. Leeds making notes on the site at Sutton Courtenay.

4

What Happened to the Britons?

'The Barbarians drive us into the sea, and the sea drives us back to the Barbarians; and between one and the other we are either slain or drowned.'

This is how Gildas, a British monk who lived in Wales or Cornwall, saw the situation in the sixth century, at a time when the Anglo-Saxons had established themselves in much of southern and eastern England. Christianity had survived from Roman times amongst the Britons in the west, and with it was retained the ability to read and write. Gildas wrote a fire-and-brimstone diatribe against the British rulers of his day blaming them and their lack of good Christian faith for the troubles which beset them. His prose is almost unreadable and it is very boring too, but just occasionally he does let slip a few facts of history, and these are doubly valuable to us today, for we can be certain that they were written down not long after they happened; Gildas died in 572 having lived through most of the sixth century.

The Barbarians whom Gildas speaks of were of course the Anglo-Saxons, and the sea was the west coast of Britain; the slaying and drowning can be dismissed as excessive exaggeration on Gildas's part. Apart from this very colourful sentence, one of the facts which Gildas records is that the Britons grouped together to form some sort of opposition to the Saxon advance. The climax of this opposition was a battle at *Mons Badonicus* which the Britons won. This battle is said to have stopped the Saxon advance for a whole generation. Strangely Gildas does not tell us the name of the leader of the British forces, but it is recorded elsewhere as Arthur.

Arthur who carried the cross of Christ for three days at Mount

Badon. Arthur who fought twelve battles and killed 960 men. Arthur of Avalon, the illustrious king. The name alone conjures up pictures of heroism and romantic knights and deeds of valour and chivalry; but all of them are fanciful. The stories are good ones, but the facts behind them are few—very few—if indeed there are any. Certainly they provide nothing solid for an archaeologist to get a spade into. Yet if there is any truth in the story of Arthur and Mount Badon, then there must be some evidence of those who were there to oppose the Saxons in the west. The search for this evidence has attracted many archaeologists in recent years.

One site of particular interest has been Cadbury Castle, the hilltop earthworks overlooking the village of South Cadbury in Somerset. Any archaeologist visiting the site would claim confidently that the earthworks were a hillfort of the pre-Roman Iron Age, dating from about 500 BC, rather than from the Age of Arthur, a thousand years later. But tradition and the antiquaries of the past have long associated Cadbury with Arthur's seat at Camelot, and although archaeologists know that Camelot is itself only a part of the romantic mythology which surrounds the name of Arthur and has no basis in fact, there was a good reason for treating the tradition with respect. Amongst sherds of pottery collected from the ploughed surface of the hill in the 1950s, there were some red and buff pieces of wheel-made pottery quite unlike the normal Iron Age and Romano-British pottery. Similar sherds are now known from a number of sites in the west of England, and in Wales and Ireland, and are recognised as being fragments of wine jars and other pottery vessels such as were in use in places bordering the Mediterranean in the fifth and sixth centuries AD. The finding of pieces of this pottery at Cadbury Castle could only mean that the hilltop had been occupied at that time.

Sherds of Mediterranean pottery found at Cadbury.

In 1966 excavations began at Cadbury under the auspices of the aptly-named Camelot Research Committee and the direction of Leslie Alcock, then a lecturer at Cardiff and now Professor of Archaeology at Glasgow University. The first year began as a trial, and three test areas were chosen for investigation, one at the back of the ramparts and two in the centre of the castle. It was quickly found that the 'castle' was indeed an Iron Age hillfort, and the massive banks and ditches which made up the ramparts had been first constructed at that time. Within the fort, too, there were extensive traces of Iron Age occupation, but this was not all, for there was also a considerable quantity of Roman material as well as a few objects which were even older than the Iron Age. Later than any of these features was a well-

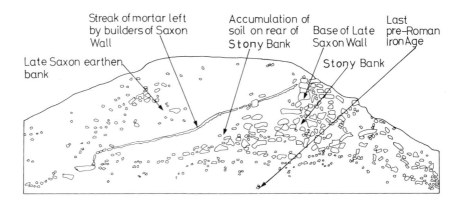

Late Saxon earthen bank

Streak of mortar left by builders of Saxon Wall

Accumulation of soil on rear of Stony Bank

Base of Late Saxon Wall

Last pre-Roman Iron Age

Stony Bank

Cross-section of the ramparts at Cadbury showing the Arthurian Stony Bank sandwiched between the Iron Age and Late Saxon defences.

built mortared wall found just under the turf on top of the rampart; but the character of its masonry made it certain that this was a late Saxon wall and not an Arthurian one. Nowhere, neither on the rampart, nor in the centre of the fort, was there any sign of features or structures of Arthurian date. The only evidence for occupation at this time was a few more sherds of the tell-tale imported Mediterranean pottery.

It was clear to members of the Camelot Research Committee that if they continued with the excavations they would find far more evidence for periods other than the age of Arthur. Yet, with careful planning, there was a reasonable chance that they would be able to find out what role the 'castle' had played during that time, and this was sufficient justification for them to proceed with the excavations. For the next four years Leslie Alcock was to direct excavations at Cadbury, on a much increased scale, over a wide area inside the fort, on one of the gateways and at numerous points around the ramparts.

Alcock's excavations at Cadbury were carried out in a blaze of publicity, and the newspapers and television closely followed the progress of the dig. The media made much of the 'Quest for Arthur' and were delighted by the finding of a gilt bronze letter A in the first season's excavations. It did not matter that the letter had come from a Roman inscription and was nothing to do with the Dark Ages; A stood for Arthur as so many journalists were anxious to point out. Some archaeologists not involved with the excavations became a little dismayed at the speculative press reports, but they need not have worried, for Alcock has revealed that his feet were firmly on the ground and that he knew all along what he was doing. His published

41

record of the evidence from the excavations is clear and precise for all to appreciate, and as for the A, Alcock writes, 'It caused an unnecessary flutter among the Arthurian romantics.'

Yet the publicity was not unwelcome; indeed it was almost necessary, for the excavation of Cadbury was no rescue excavation carried out in advance of a new housing development or a new motorway which could be financed by a grant from the Department of the Environment. There was no 'threat' to the site, and the full cost of the excavation had to be raised by the Camelot Research Committee. Publicity at all levels was one of the ways of doing this, and the excavations were financed by the contributions of many people from the learned societies to the newspapers, as well as by the many thousands of interested people who climbed up to the top of Cadbury Castle to see for themselves.

The story which emerges from the five years of excavations at Cadbury is one of human settlement and activity, life and death, on the hilltop over a period of 4,000 years. Had Alcock chosen to explore merely a part of this story, had he chosen to investigate just the fifth and sixth centuries, he would have been lost—for he would have had no chance of identifying the features of that date without the sequence which the excavation of all periods made plain to him. This is one of the lessons of South Cadbury—while historians may be able to go straight to the written documents which illustrate their period, an archaeologist must be able to dig his way through other periods to discover the true facts about that period which most interests him.

The sequence at Cadbury begins with Neolithic pottery of the fourth millennium BC; then follows late Neolithic and early Bronze Age material of about 2,500–2,000 BC, followed again by pottery of the late Bronze Age and early Iron Age, 800–600 BC. It was in the Iron Age, from 600 BC onwards, that the ramparts around the top of the hill were first constructed, and subsequently remodelled several times. At the end of the Iron Age, in the first century AD, the site, as a tribal centre of the Durotriges, met the fate of so many of those who opposed the invading Roman armies; it was attacked and captured and there was evidence of a massacre at a date some time in the '70s AD. After this there is very little evidence for actual use during the Roman period, save that in the fourth century it seems likely that the hilltop was the site of a pagan Roman temple. This is where the letter A fits in; it is the sort of piece which was used in nailing up dedicatory inscriptions, and several similar letters are known from other temple sites. There then follows a phase illustrated by the most fugitive of

remains. The banks of the rampart had been raised by a number of stony layers at some date between the Roman period and the later refortification of the site under Aethelred the Unready (978–1016). This refortification is suggested by coins of Aethelred on which the mint name Cadanbyrig (Cadbury) is clearly struck, and is confirmed by the discovery of a well-built mortared wall in the top layers of the surrounding ramparts.

Working down from the top and up from the bottom there was a gap between the Iron Age banks and the Aethelredan banks which was filled only with the stony layers which Alcock labelled the Stony Bank. Its filling contained Roman debris, so it was late Roman at the earliest; but its date was eventually pushed—with certainty—into the fifth century by the finding of a very late Roman coin in its makeup. The coin bore the name of Honorius who was emperor from AD 393 to 402, and one of the last Roman emperors whose coins are found in Britain. It began to look as though the Stony Bank might represent a refortification of Cadbury in the Dark Ages.

In places the Stony Bank was found to have a retaining wall in the front, and this survived particularly well on either side of the gateway. Here the bank and wall were found to have been interlaced with timber beams. The ends of the bank were shored up with planks, and the gate itself was based on four massive timber posts which were bedded deeply into the solid rock. In the gateway were found two sill beams some three metres apart, showing that the gate had been a really substantial affair. There was a quite distinct roadway leading up to the gate and lying on this, amongst other things, there was a silver ring-shaped buckle with ornament of Anglo-Saxon type dating to the sixth century. The buckle was covered up with the layers of a roadway which was associated with the gate. Here, then, was certain evidence that the roadway and hence the gate had been in use in the sixth century. This tied in well with the scatter of imported pottery of the same sort of date which had been found in the surface soil.

The search within the circuit of the defences was no less intense, but despite the scatter of finds, all traces of a building that could definitely be associated with this phase proved elusive until the 1969 season of excavations. During this year, amongst the mosaic of pits and post holes which littered the site, a number of large post holes were found all filled with the same sort of soil; when linked together it was seen that they produced the outline of a large rectangular building, and thanks to a sherd of the all-important Mediterranean pottery crammed into one of the holes this building too can reasonably be

Ring-shaped silver buckle with Anglo-Saxon ornament found on the surface of the road leading to the Arthurian gate at Cadbury.

White pegs indicating the post holes of a large rectangular building of the Arthurian period at Cadbury.

dated to the age of Arthur. The outline plan measured nineteen metres long by ten metres wide and was divided up inside by two rows of smaller posts, so that the building must have been like an enormous timber barn with three aisles. The surface of the ground has been so abraded at this point that there is no trace of the level of the floor of the building and even some of the post holes had disappeared; one can only guess at the appearance of the superstructure, but the size, and the date, point to this as the remains of one of the chief buildings on the site during the Arthurian period.

For Cadbury, Leslie Alcock's five years of arduous excavations have revealed a lengthy history of which just a part relates to the age of Arthur. The excavations have not shown that Arthur held court at Cadbury, nor that he even visited the place—indeed, how could they? But they have shown that the hilltop was occupied at the time, and that the occupation involved an extensive renewal of the fortifications and gates and the building of at least one enormous timber hall. It seems unlikely that this was put up for a single summer's campaign; it is far more likely that Cadbury Castle was a secure and permanent fortress—a base from which to plan campaigns and a safe refuge in times of danger.

It is tempting to try to relate the Arthurian period at Cadbury Castle to the political events of the day, so far as these are known or may be guessed at. Was this the main centre for British resistance to

45

Anglo-Saxon gilt bronze saucer brooch found in excavations at Cadbury.

the Saxon advance? Or were there other similar fortified sites which have yet to be recognised? This we must wait to find out. What the excavations at Cadbury have shown very clearly is that archaeological evidence of the Britons in the Dark Ages is very elusive, and that even such a major work as Cadbury cannot be recognised without long and most meticulous excavation. This certainly poses problems for archaeologists seeking the humbler settlements which we must suppose the ordinary Britons to have lived in.

There can be no doubt that at times during the fifth and sixth centuries Cadbury Castle was the scene of very great activity, and for this reason it is all the more remarkable that so few British objects have been found there. Ironically, the only two decorated objects of this period are Anglo-Saxon, the ring-like buckle found under the surface of the road going through the gateway and a small gilt bronze saucer brooch with a face mask on it. One almost gets the impression that the British made no objects at all; but this of course is not true. One particular skill which did survive the collapse of Roman Britain was enamelling on bronze, and during the sixth and seventh centuries British workshops produced a splendid series of bronze bowls with enamelled decoration on them. These bowls are known as hanging bowls, for in place of handles they have three rings by which they were suspended, probably on a sort of tripod. It seems likely that these bowls were made at many places; they are the sort of industry which is portable, with an itinerant craftsman, like a tinker, taking his tools and equipment with him and setting to work wherever there is a demand. No doubt it was its portable nature which enabled this craft to survive.

Evidence of the manufacture of these bowls and related objects has been found at several sites; chiefly it takes the form of bronze-casting debris and discarded crucibles. Alcock himself found considerable evidence of such industry in his excavations at the fort of Dinas Powys in South Wales. But apart from the manufacturing debris there are few traces of the finished products on British sites. These come mostly from Anglo-Saxon graves, and it is clear that the Anglo-Saxons admired the British bowls and were eager to acquire them.

By a quirk of history, it happens that the only decorated metal object yet found on the site of the Anglo-Saxon village at Chalton is an enamelled disc from a British hanging bowl. The design on this disc is one of the favourite motifs of the hanging bowl craftsmen. It is a whirl of spirals which forms an almost perfect pattern neatly fitting into a circle. This pattern was never used by the early Anglo-Saxon metalworkers, who preferred their own dismembered or interwoven animal designs; and the two traditions remained distinct and separate. But in the seventh and eighth centuries, when it came to choosing patterns to illustrate the holy manuscript copies of the gospels such as the Book of Durrow and the Lindisfarne Gospels, the monkish illustrators adapted elements from both traditions, incorporating the design of the enamelled spirals and the interlacing animals and developing both together into intricate and harmonious patterns. It is probably in this form that the British contribution to later Anglo-Saxon art is most familiar.

Bronze bowl of British manufacture, showing probable method of suspension.

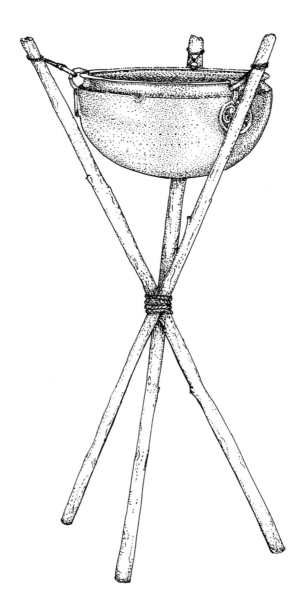

5

Sutton Hoo-a King's Grave

Many landowners have archaeological sites on their property, but few such sites are as prominent as the group of barrows at Sutton Hoo in Suffolk. Some fifteen large mounds are clustered together on top of the hill slope overlooking the River Deben opposite Woodbridge, near Ipswich. Many of them have hollows in the top — a sure sign that they have been plundered in the past; but there is no record of when this was done nor of what was found. It would be natural for any landowner to be curious, and Mrs Edith May Pretty was no exception. So, in 1938, she decided to investigate the barrows.

On the advice of the Ipswich Museum, Mrs Pretty hired the services of Basil Brown, a local amateur archaeologist, and during the summer he opened three of the barrows. Two of them contained cremations; and though both of them had been opened before, one still contained a burial deposit which was more or less intact. The third mound was found to have contained a burial in a boat; this grave like the others had been robbed, and the boat had disintegrated. Only a few rusted nails were left to show where it had once been. The grave robbers had taken away nearly all the valuable objects but there remained enough in the way of broken fragments to show that all three barrows were early Anglo-Saxon, of the sixth and seventh centuries. Although nothing much to look at, the finds were sufficiently interesting for the authorities of the Ipswich Museum to encourage Mrs Pretty to continue work the following year.

Basil Brown began work again on May 8th, 1939. Mrs Pretty directed him to the largest barrow which was some thirty metres across and stood nearly three metres high at its centre. Within a few days he had come across rows of rusted iron nails embedded in the

The shape of the boat at Sutton Hoo.

sandy soil exactly like those he had found in the disturbed boat burial the year before; he realised that he was dealing with another boat, and from then on proceeded with great care. All trace of the timber of the boat had disappeared, but where it had been the sand was stained dark brown in contrast to its normal yellow, and the dark-stained sand was harder than the yellow. By carefully removing the yellow sand from the inside of the boat and leaving the discoloured sand and the rusted iron rivets in place, Basil Brown was able to discover the exact shape and lines of the boat.

After more than a month the work was nearing the centre of the boat and the excavation was getting daily more complicated. Basil Brown had started on the east side of the mound, on what was eventually found to be the bows of the boat, and as he proceeded in towards the centre the boat widened out till it was eventually four and a half metres across the beam. This meant that an enormous part of the covering mound had to be dug away, and the sides had continually to be cut back to prevent the soft sand from slipping down into the partially excavated boat. At one point near the centre of the mound

49

Brown came upon some pieces of sixteenth-century pottery at the bottom of a pit. It looked as though someone else had tried to get into the mound four hundred years ago; but their pit had not reached the boat, and Brown calculated that they had abandoned the attempt.

As his two helpers worked away on the mound above, Brown concentrated on cleaning out the boat. He was conscious that he was approaching the centre of it and he had every reason to believe that the burial deposit would be intact. On June 14th, he recorded in his diary:

'After tea I came back alone and worked hard, and then came the first find, a large iron ring and what appeared to be a smaller one close by and with my hands I carefully cleaned away the sand above using a soft brush . . . Then green of [corroded] bronze bands, or what appeared to be bronze bands, showed up and what was undoubtedly wood which gave out a hollow sound.'

Basil Brown did not immediately rush to dig out the burial deposit, and for the next few days he concentrated on cutting back the mound. But meanwhile the archaeological world was buzzing with excitement at the news first of the discovery of the boat, and now at the prospect of a burial deposit which was undisturbed. Experts came to visit the site from the British Museum and the Office of Works and there was much discussion as to how the burial deposit should be tackled. Basil Brown confided in his diary, 'This find has certainly caused a big stir in the antiquarian world.' Eventually it was decided that Basil Brown should proceed with the clearing of the boat while the burial deposit itself was excavated by a team of experienced archaeologists under Mr C. W. Phillips. Even for them this was to be no easy task, for nothing like it had ever before been found in England.

Phillips and his team worked around the burial deposit, gradually removing the sand and uncovering the tops of the objects buried in the centre of the boat. They found traces of timber walls across the boat at both ends of the deposit suggesting that a hut or cabin, some five and a half metres long, had been erected as a burial chamber in the centre of the boat. Once the edge of the deposit had been located they were able to move in to begin uncovering the objects which were projecting through the sand. On July 20th, a large silver dish was located in the centre of the boat; it was covered with wood and was thought at first to be a shield, so it was left in place and the uncovering went on around it. On the next day two small pyramid-shaped gold studs set with garnets were found further west, and the following day

W.F. Grimes at work in the burial chamber uncovering the iron cauldron chain.

a whole series of gold objects—an enormous gold buckle, jewelled belt fittings, a jewelled purse lid and a quantity of gold coins. Alongside these lay the rusted remains of an iron sword with a most elaborate garnet-studded gold handle. Between the silver dish and this cluster of jewellery was a collection of drinking vessels, horns and wooden cups, all fitted with decorated metal rims; and below the silver dish when that was lifted the following week were more silver vessels, a ladle and a fluted bowl, two bronze hanging bowls and another group of wooden cups with metal rims, all sitting on what looked like two stuffed leather cushions. Across the ends of the burial chamber the objects were simply piled one upon another. At the west end was an enormous iron standard, more bronze bowls, an iron-bound tub, a pile of silver bowls and two spoons, a cluster of spearheads and other weapons, a massive whetstone with metal fittings and a host of fragments of gold leaf and small gilt fittings which really did come from a shield; an elaborate shield boss lay below them. Beside this there were the remains of a helmet which had once been a splendidly ornamented object but was now crushed into hundreds of pieces. At the other end of the chamber was another large iron-bound tub and a row of iron cauldrons together with a long and

51

intricately made cauldron chain — these were the objects which Basil Brown had located first over a month before.

Basil Brown's careful beginning had paved the way for a week of the most spectacular discoveries by Phillips and his helpers. In the words of O.G.S.Crawford, the archaeological officer of the Ordnance Survey, who was one of those taking part, 'It is the finest archaeological find ever made in Great Britain.' Crawford has recorded something of the excitement of those few hectic days. 'An archaeologist can get an intellectual thrill from discoveries such as postholes and potsherds that may mean nothing to the man in the street; but he is also sufficiently human, usually, to enjoy a successful treasure hunt as much as anyone.' Clearly Crawford had enjoyed himself; he went on,

'In the Saxon ship were buried, amid much else, gold and silver worth a fortune. But it was not mere useless bullion like the bank reserves of modern states; it consisted of objects of great artistic value. As we watched emerging daily from the earth things that we saw were unique we felt that we were present at the unveiling of history, and that the history of our own country. There were great moments that none of us who were present will ever forget — such as the lifting of the silver plate that for days had lain there half covering a silver basin. We knew that exciting things were waiting for the uncovering — and when the great moment came we were not disappointed. The finding of the gold clasps was another wonderful moment. As always with gold objects they were in perfect condition without spot or tarnish. They are unique and it was a happy chance that they should be found on a day when we had visitors from the British Museum. The same evening there came as a fitting climax to a crowded day, what was perhaps the most unexpected discovery of all. For some time we had been puzzled by a tantalising patch of purple dust, sure harbinger of silver. It developed into a dome-shaped lump which Mr Grimes undercut and lifted out on a tray. He deposited this on the grass outside the barrow and proceeded to take away the much corroded outer fragments. When at last he lifted the top we saw a bright silver bowl, base upwards, in perfect condition, and under this was yet another bowl. In all eight were thus uncovered, each with different ornamentation inside. Each day of that exciting week yielded some first rate find, often of a type unknown before. As we worked along the keel we *knew* that under those mouldy-looking lumps of decayed wood lay hidden things of priceless historic and artistic value. We anticipated the finding of the sword, shield, helmet and drinking horns and we were not disappointed. But many other things we had not expected—the purse, the silver bowls and tray, for instance, and later the axe and the suit of chainmail.'

But amidst the excitement of finding all these things there arose a question which became more important as the excavation proceeded. There was never any doubt that all the objects were part of a burial deposit—but where was the burial? No trace of a body could be found anywhere.

The excavations were completed late in August 1939. Because of the presence of gold and silver a coroner's court was called to decide on the ownership of the find. The jury decided that Mrs Pretty, who had instigated the excavation, was the finder and the legal owner of the objects. With great generosity she then donated them to the nation, and they were transferred to the British Museum. But, no sooner had the objects reached the British Museum, than they had to be packed away again for safe keeping during the war. It was not till after the war that serious study of the treasure could begin; it has been going on almost continuously ever since.

Despite the lack of a body, there has never been any doubt that this was the burial deposit of a king. The great early English epic poem *Beowulf* which was written about AD 700, begins with a description of

The jewelled purse lid.

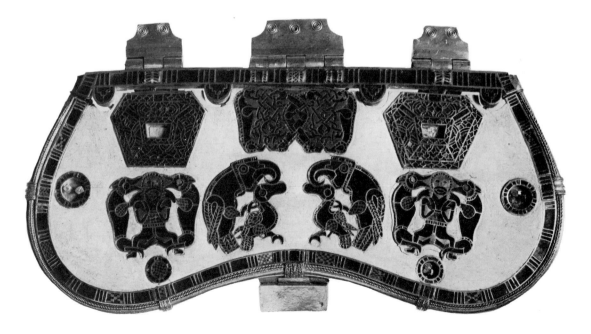

the funeral of the Danish king Scyld; but the description might almost be that of the Sutton Hoo burial itself. It reads:

> Then Scyld departed at the destined hour,
> that powerful man sought the Lord's protection.
> His own close companions carried him
> down to the sea, as he, lord of the Danes,
> had asked while he could still speak.
> That well-loved man had ruled his land for many years.
> There in harbour stood the ring-prowed ship,
> the prince's vessel, icy, eager to sail;
> and then they laid their dear lord,
> the giver of rings, deep within the ship
> by the mast in majesty; many treasures
> and adornments from far and wide were gathered there.
> I have never heard of a ship equipped
> more handsomely with weapons and war-gear,
> swords and corslets; on his breast
> lay countless treasures that were to travel far
> with him into the waves' domain.

The only difference between Scyld's burial and Sutton Hoo is that Scyld's boat was pushed out to sea to go wherever the wind took it, while the Sutton Hoo boat was dragged ashore to be buried under a massive barrow.

In size and wealth the Sutton Hoo treasure far exceeds that of every other Anglo-Saxon grave in the whole of England; the objects in it are evidence of its owner's widespread connections. From the nearby west of Britain there are three hanging bowls; the largest is most elaborately decorated with both round and square scroll-ornamented enamelled plaques around the outside, and inside there is a bronze fish spotted with enamel and set up on a pedestal in the centre of the bowl as though it is swimming. This is certainly the most exotic hanging bowl known from anywhere. From the extreme east, from the Byzantine world, come the silver vessels, the nest of bowls, the ladle, the fluted bowl and the great silver dish. This is stamped with the control marks of the Emperor Anastasius. There is a cast bronze bowl from Egypt. The coins are all Merovingian; they were minted at various places in France and Belgium and the Rhineland. The shield and helmet are from Sweden, and perhaps the sword too; though not the jewelled pyramidal studs, nor the jewelled belt fittings, nor the purse lid. These pieces cannot be matched elsewhere. The making of

54

The bronze hanging bowl decorated with enamelled plaques and an enamel-spotted fish on a pedestal in the centre.

this jewellery involved the cutting and shaping and polishing of thousands of garnets and their arrangement in the most ambitious and complicated gold settings—these objects must surely be the work of the king's own jewellers. The great gold buckle is another unique object; it is 13 cms long and solid gold—it weighs nearly half a kilo—decorated with a knotlike pattern of interlacing animal bodies. This too must be a product of the king's own workshops. Perhaps the strangest object in the whole treasure is the whetstone. It is a massive four-sided bar of fine-grained stone carved at each end with four faces; the knobbed ends of the stone are surrounded by bronze cages, and one is topped with a twisted iron ring surmounted by a bronze stag. The complete object measures nearly a metre and weighs almost three kilos. But it has never been used to sharpen anything; it is too large and too heavy, and the edges are unmarked. The object has more the appearance of a ceremonial than a functional thing, and it is for this reason that it has been called a sceptre, a symbol of kingly power and perhaps also possessed of magical powers and religious significance.

The Sutton Hoo burial contains so many different sorts of object that it is more than one man can do to interpret them all, and it is not surprising that many scholars have played a part. Naturally one of the first questions they have tried to answer has been, whose grave was this? The first attempt to answer this question, as early as 1940, was made by the late H. M. Chadwick, a most distinguished Anglo-Saxon historian. His argument went like this: the burial is undoubtedly pagan, for no Christian king would have been buried in this way. Yet, within the boat, amongst the objects of Byzantine silver, were two spoons which suggest that the man was nominally a Christian. The spoons are each inscribed with a name, one Saul, the other Paul. Now Paul, it will be remembered, is the name taken by Saul after his dramatic conversion on the road to Damascus. A pair of spoons bearing these two names is then an appropriate symbol of conversion; they are the sort of objects which might have been given to a man at his baptism. Thus it appears we should be looking for a king who had been baptised as a Christian but who had lapsed back into his heathen ways, or perhaps had never actually forsaken them. Amongst the kings of East Anglia in the seventh century, there is just such a man; his name was Raedwald and he died about AD 625. In his *Ecclesiastical History* Bede comments on Raedwald's religious practices, 'He was baptised as a Christian in Kent; but it was in vain, for when he got home his wife and advisers persuaded him against it . . . he seemed to be serving both Christ and his pagan gods, for in the same temple he had one altar for Christian worship and another for his pagan practices.' Chadwick carefully considered the names of the other kings of East Anglia in the seventh century, but none fits so well as Raedwald.

Chadwick's choice of Raedwald was rejected early on, for the numismatists who studied the coins said that 625 was an impossibly early date. Various other dates were suggested; most of them were around AD 650, but none of the kings who died around this date seemed as appropriate as Raedwald had been. Another complication was the lack of a body in the grave. The excavators had looked carefully for some evidence of bones, or at least of teeth, but they had found none, and Phillips concluded that there had never been a body in the grave. To account for this Phillips proposed that the whole barrow should be thought of as a cenotaph—a monument for a king

The ceremonial whetstone.

56

who had died and been buried elsewhere. So much was unique about the burial that this new proposal was readily accepted. The dating of the coins and the cenotaph theory have given rise to continued speculation as to who was being commemorated here. Various suggestions were made: was the monument perhaps to a king who was killed in battle and whose body was never recovered, or was it a pagan monument put up by the pagan followers of a king who had become a Christian and had been buried in a church? Within this range of possibilities almost all the East Anglian kings of the seventh century have had their supporters at one time or another.

One of the silver spoons.

Within the British Museum the Sutton Hoo treasure is the special responsibility of Dr Rupert Bruce-Mitford and his team of research workers. In recent years they have been working systematically through the finds in preparation for their complete publication. In particular their attention has concentrated on the shield and the helmet. Both were in hundreds of pieces when found and they remained that way till they could be reconstructed after the war. During the twenty years in which they have become familiar to so many people these reconstructions have also raised a number of problems. The general idea of the helmet as an iron cap with a facemask, cheek pieces and neck guard all decorated with embossed bronze sheeting was well established, but the size of the helmet and the actual shape of some of the pieces was open to discussion. For example it was noticed, by no less a person than Her Majesty the Queen when she visited the Sutton Hoo treasure at the British Museum, that the mask protecting the face actually rested on the bridge of the nose in an impossibly uncomfortable position. So in 1971 it was decided to dismantle the helmet completely, to re-examine all the fragments which survived and then to attempt a new reconstruction. The helmet is a Swedish object and the only comparable helmets come from graves in Sweden; these helmets were also examined to see what light they could throw on the probable shape of the Sutton Hoo helmet.

The new reconstruction presents a most impressive object. It is like a large crash helmet with a curving guard projecting down over the back of the neck and a decorated visor with eye holes covering the front of the face. At each side are hinged cheek pieces which can be fastened together under the chin. An inlaid crest over the top of the helmet ends in dragon heads, and the nose and eyebrows resemble the body and spread wings of another dragon. The inside was fitted out with a padded lining to fit comfortably over the head.

Exhibited alongside the reconstruction in the British Museum is a replica of the helmet made in the Royal Armouries of the Tower of London. It is a faithful copy of the original. 'The chief impact of the replica,' writes Dr Bruce-Mitford, 'is that we have, in contrast to the drab brown construction into which the original fragments are rebuilt, a shining white object. The bare iron is only exposed in segments here and there, but the burnished natural metal comes up to a bright silver colour, while the decorated bronze foil plates which cover the rest of the helmet's surface are tinned.' Having tried on this replica myself, my own impression—apart from the weight which I think one would get used to—is that the wearer is blinkered. When the cheek pieces are fastened you can see nothing at all at the sides and can only see forward through the eye holes at the front. This might have been sufficient when fighting a single opponent, but in the melée of a battle the wearer would have been terribly vulnerable to attack from the sides.

The shield, like the helmet, has been taken to pieces and reconstructed. It is now revealed as a circle of wood a metre in diameter covered with calf skin and decorated with elaborate dragons and birds in gilt bronze and gold foil. It too is a Swedish object. Comparable shields and helmets from Sweden come like the Sutton Hoo examples from boat graves situated chiefly at Vendel and Valsgärde north of Uppsala in central Sweden. This is of the very greatest interest and significance, for this area of Sweden is the only place other than East Anglia where there were boat burials at this time. There is thus a very close link between the burial ground at Sutton Hoo and central Sweden, and it looks very much as though the royal house of East Anglia may have had its origin in Sweden. There is no hint of this connection in Bede or in other historical writings though it could explain why the epic *Beowulf* tells what is really a Scandinavian story.

In 1966 Bruce-Mitford returned to Sutton Hoo to re-open the barrow. When the excavations were completed in 1939, the ship had been filled with bracken, and during the war years the area had been used as a tank training ground. Fortunately the ship was little damaged and Bruce Mitford found it possible to re-expose the outlines of the timbers. The whole of the inside of the ship was then cast in plaster, in numerous sections, so that there is now a permanent record of the shape of the ship, and perhaps one day a replica of it will be made.

Besides the study of the ship, one of Bruce-Mitford's reasons for

reopening the barrow was to try to answer the question about the lack of a body. Obviously, if the 1939 excavators had not found one, there would not be one there in 1966; but it was hoped that chemical tests applied to the soil would show whether there had been one there originally or not. Acid soil such as the sand at Sutton Hoo is capable of destroying and obliterating all traces of a body, but the disintegration of the bones results in an artificially high phosphate content in the surrounding soil. Tests on the soil beneath the burial chamber showed that it did have a higher phosphate content than was normal in the sandy soil, but there was no definite concentration indicating the position or presence of a body. However, the same sort of tests were applied to some of the objects from the burial, and it was found that the rusted iron of the sword had absorbed an unusually high quantity of phosphate. It looks then as though some source rich in phosphates had lain alongside the sword . . . and this is exactly the position in which a body would have been expected, with the most lavish jewellery being worn or laid out on top of it. The results of these tests make it as certain as it is now possible to be that there was originally a body in the grave. In this sense, then, the Sutton Hoo barrow is an ordinary burial and the cenotaph theory can be forgotten.

There remain the coins. It has always been hoped that they would provide a firm date for the burial and allow certain identification of the king, rather than be the source of many conflicting theories. But Merovingian coins are very difficult to date. It is only very seldom that they have a king's name on them. Normally one side bears the name of the moneyer and the other the place where they were minted. There were thirty-seven coins in the purse at Sutton Hoo and only one of them had a king's name on it; this was the Frankish king Theodebert II who reigned from AD 595 to 612. To decide the date of the other coins in the purse it is necessary to compare the style and decoration of those which have no dates with other coins which are dated. But this is a subjective method, and it depends on people's opinions rather than on certain facts; that is why it is so difficult to get agreement. In 1960 new work by the French numismatist Jean Lafaurie suggested that the date of the group of coins from Sutton Hoo was nearer 625 than the date of 650 which was the one usually preferred. This suggestion was of crucial importance and it resulted in a numismatist from the British Museum, Dr John Kent, being asked to investigate the whole problem again. Dr Kent's work has involved a complete reworking of the whole system of Merovingian coinage, and then checking his results by analysis of the gold content of many of the pieces. His final result is an emphatic confirmation of Lafaurie's suggestion. He sums up his lengthy argument in this way, 'I have no hesitation in concluding that *c*.620–625 is the date when the latest coin to enter the Sutton Hoo purse was minted.'

So the wheel has turned full circle, and we can come back to Professor Chadwick's original assertion that the barrow is the grave of Raedwald. This is something on which most scholars now agree.

Raedwald was the last great pagan king of East Anglia. There, as in other parts of England, the seventh century saw permanent conversion to Christianity, first of the royal families and then of their followers and the rest of the people. Christian kings were buried in churches as was Aethelbert of Kent, the first English king to be converted; he died in 616 and was buried in St Martin's chapel at St Peter and St Paul's church at Canterbury. Lesser folk were buried outside the churches in the surrounding churchyards. This was to be the custom for the future.

6

The Anglo-Saxon Church

There are Anglo-Saxon churches still in use all over England. Other Anglo-Saxon buildings were in wood, but wood rots eventually and the buildings were pulled down and replaced. Churches, like town walls, were built in stone and lasted and although the town walls have long since ceased to have any use and they too have now disappeared, the churches have remained, for they have been in constant use and have been cared for and maintained by successive generations.

Inevitably these Anglo-Saxon churches have been altered and added to so that in many cases they are now unrecognisable. A few—a mere handful—survive more or less as they were built, but the rest have been modified to such an extent that now only a few pieces of an original door or window, or the corner stones of a wall survive to indicate the great age of the original building.

Finding the Anglo-Saxon parts of a church is not always easy, but it is an interesting and stimulating exercise. For many years now it has been the hobby of Dr H. M. Taylor. Back in the 1930s he and his wife began visiting the churches which were said to be of Anglo-Saxon origin; they took to recording their visits and to measuring and drawing the buildings, so that over the years they have compiled a comprehensive record of all surviving remains of Anglo-Saxon churches. Now, after a full career as a university lecturer and administrator, Dr Taylor has retired, and his hobby has become his full-time activity. He and his wife have already produced two large books containing their descriptions of all Anglo-Saxon churches, and he is now at work on a third book which will analyse all the information which he has recorded.

In making their records the Taylors had first to decide what was

The north wall of the nave at Geddington, Northamptonshire.

Anglo-Saxon and what was not. That may sound simple; after all there are numerous books on architecture which describe the characteristics of the Anglo-Saxon period, but as Dr Taylor has shown, so often what is said is merely the opinion of an expert, and even experts can be wrong. So he has looked at each building afresh. His approach has been a very archaeological one, for he has studied the development of each building to see which parts are original and which are later additions, in what order the various additions have

63

been made, and so on. Medieval styles of architecture from the Conquest onwards, Norman, Early English, Decorated and Perpendicular, are easily recognised, and can be dated by reference to churches whose dates are well known from documents. But this is not so for Anglo-Saxon churches; there are only half a dozen or so for which Dr Taylor is prepared to give a firm date on the basis of direct documentary evidence, and these in no way give a complete picture of the various Anglo-Saxon styles of architecture. However, once he has recorded the complete history of each building and established the sequence in which it was built, it follows that all parts which are older than the Norman period must be Anglo-Saxon.

One of the prime examples of the value of Dr Taylor's method comes from Geddington in Northamptonshire. Here the church was enlarged in Norman times, an aisle was added to the north side of the nave and a series of Norman arches were inserted into the former nave wall. It is possible to see on the outer face of the wall that the construction of the arches cut away part of a window; this was blocked up but the undisturbed part of its framework has remained in position. It is obvious that the window must have been there before the arch was built, so the window must be Anglo-Saxon. But that is not the end of the story, for the window itself can be seen to interrupt a line of decorative stonework—an arrangement of triangular-headed arches on the outside of the wall. So the decorative stonework must be earlier than the window. There are thus two periods of Anglo-Saxon building here, an original wall with a band of decorative stonework, into which was inserted a small window with a large monolithic head.

An even more certain example of Anglo-Saxon dating comes when the various parts of a building are piled on top of one another as in a tower. The tower of the church of St Peter at Monkwearmouth is a good example of this. It stands eighteen metres high, and it is all Anglo-Saxon. The upper half of it belongs to the latest phase of Anglo-Saxon architecture, shortly before the Conquest; the lower half is more complicated. In it Dr Taylor has identified three different phases of building, each adding a bit to the height of the tower. The lowest part was not built as a tower at all but merely as a porch at the west end of the nave. The walls of this porch are only fifty centimetres thick and can never have been intended to carry the massive tower which they do today. It is incredible that it has survived intact.

If the upper half of the tower dates from the period around the Norman Conquest, then the lower parts must be older, though the architectural sequence by itself cannot give any clue as to how much

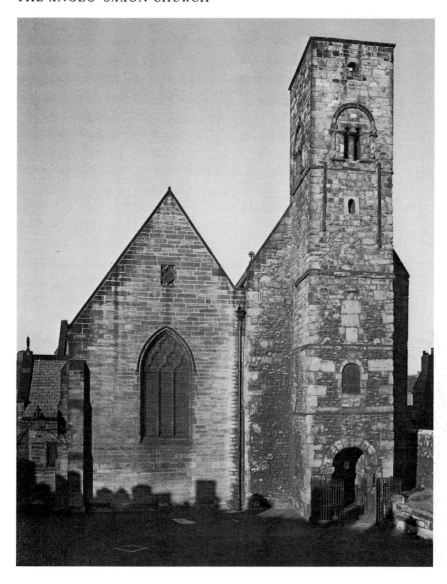

The tower of St Peter's church at Monkwearmouth.

older. In fact, in this case, it is probable that the lower parts are much earlier, and that the lowest stage is amongst the earliest pieces of Anglo-Saxon building surviving in this country, for the church at Monkwearmouth was part of a monastery which had been founded back in the seventh century.

Monkwearmouth, on the north bank of the River Wear opposite Sunderland, and Jarrow, a few miles away on the south bank of the Tyne, were two monasteries founded by the Northumbrian nobleman Benedict Biscop. Throughout their early years they were very closely associated with one another; Bede described them as 'one

Fragment of a turned stone baluster shaft from Monkwearmouth.

monastery in two places' and he should have known, for they were his home. Bede's own writings are an indication of the influence of these monasteries, for he was not a traveller and it was here that he was able to read and study the books which provided him with his inspiration and his source material. It is unlikely that there was anywhere else in England at this time where he could have found such learning, and this was due almost entirely to Benedict Biscop.

As a young man Biscop had travelled abroad, staying in various monasteries in France and even visiting Rome several times. He decided that he would found a monastery that was comparable to those he had seen on his travels, and Bede records that from the first

66

he wanted to build a proper stone church. Since there were no builders and masons in England who knew how to build one, he himself went to France to find craftsmen who could do the job for him. Within a year the church was built and the roof was on, but there were still no windows. Biscop wanted proper glass windows, so he sent again to France for glaziers. When the church was finally complete and the life of the monastery established, he went abroad again, this time to Rome. From there he brought back a large number of books and sacred relics and pictures for the walls of the church, and also a choirmaster who would teach his community to sing.

Just a little of the extraordinary nature of these two monasteries has been brought to light by the recent excavations of Professor Rosemary Cramp of Durham University. The original churches, now much altered, are still in use at both Monkwearmouth and Jarrow. Nevertheless, Professor Cramp has been able to excavate large areas at both sites, exploring the buildings located on the south side of the churches. Many of these have proved to be medieval, but some parts of stone buildings of Saxon date have been found in both excavations. The largest of these is at Jarrow where the foundations of a rectangular building twenty-eight metres long by eight metres wide have been uncovered. This seems to be some of the work which was inspired if not actually carried out by Biscop's imported masons; the walls were solidly built on a cobble and clay foundation in courses of small stones with large stone corner blocks. The floor was made of concrete laid on a bed of small stones and surfaced with powdered brick which gave it a pinkish surface. This was a technique which dated back to Roman times and had not been seen in England since the fourth century.

The buildings at Monkwearmouth were more fragmentary and cannot easily be interpreted, though they have produced a mass of debris showing that the same sort of builders had worked here too. Amongst the debris were slabs of crushed-brick concrete flooring, lumps of plaster from the walls, fragments of stone strips like the one that had formed the decorative work at Geddington and pieces of turned stone balusters such as are to be seen in position on either side of the doorway at the bottom of the tower. There are also many fragments of glass—shining evidence of the work of Biscop's glaziers. They are not mere plain pieces, but come in a whole range of colours—pale blue, dark blue, blue-green, emerald green, olive green, yellow-brown, amber and red. Most of these fragments are broken, but one survives intact; it is triangular with the edges chipped

A complete triangular 'quarry' of honey-coloured glass with white trails from Monkwearmouth.

OPPOSITE
Excavations in pro-
gress in 1966 alongside
the cathedral at Win-
chester.

to shape. The glass is honey-coloured and is embellished additionally with opaque white trails which have been 'combed' like slipware pottery. It measures only eight centimetres long. None of the fragments were larger than this and to make up windows they were fastened together with H-shaped strips of lead, several of which were found. It is apparent that the windows were not ordinary clear glass but highly coloured, and no doubt highly patterned, stained glass ones.

Professor Cramp's excavations have shown a little of what Biscop's craftsmen could produce, and of the surroundings of the monasteries where Bede lived and worked. Jarrow and Monkwearmouth are among the earliest examples of Anglo-Saxon architecture, and it was from buildings like them that the later styles were to develop. The two monastery churches are not vast, and it is probable that many larger buildings were built in subsequent years in other parts of the country. But of these, the greater Anglo-Saxon churches, we have now almost no trace, for they were in their turn replaced with new and yet larger buildings in the eleventh and twelfth centuries.

This was brought home to me most impressively in 1965 when I was involved in excavations on the Augustinian Abbey at Cirencester. The Abbey had been built in the twelfth century but below its foundations were discovered the remains of an earlier church of Anglo-Saxon date. This was totally unexpected, but what was even more surprising was its size. The church was fifty-five metres long, which is larger not only than Jarrow and Monkwearmouth but also than every other surviving Anglo-Saxon church . . . and this was a building for which there is not one single documentary reference recorded anywhere. Cirencester itself has little claim to fame in later Saxon times, and the reason for so large a building is not known; but if one can turn up so unexpectedly, what must have been lost of the better known and recorded churches? This question has been answered by the recent excavations at Winchester carried out by Martin Biddle, the director of the Winchester Research Unit.

The cathedral at Winchester is a Norman building; it was consecrated on St Swithun's day 1093, and on that day St Swithun's throne was brought from the old church, the Old Minster, into the new cathedral. On the following day workmen began to pull down the old church, and there is now no trace of it above ground. The documentary evidence suggests that the Old Minster was situated to the north of the cathedral, so it was here that Martin Biddle looked for it.

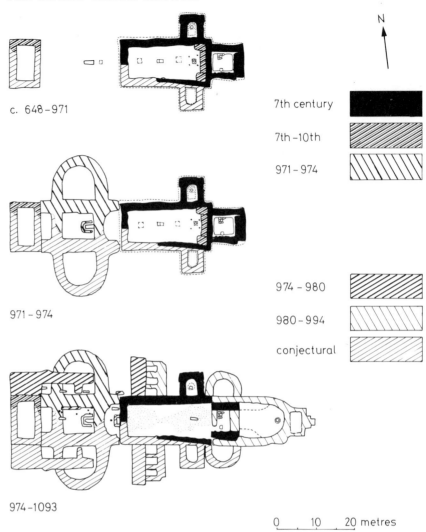

c. 648–971

7th century

7th–10th

971–974

971–974

974–980

980–994

conjectural

974–1093

0   10   20 metres

The development of the Old Minster at Winchester as interpreted from the excavations.

In 1962 the Dean and Chapter of the cathedral gave permission for excavations to be carried out in the green lawns of the Cathedral Close, and the first exploratory trenches were dug out from the Cathedral walls. The upper layers were found to be full of graves dating back as early as the twelfth century but not earlier, and below that were signs of robbed foundations, indicating substantial walls that looked as though they could have belonged to the Old Minster.

These initial finds were sufficient to justify continuing the work, and for a further seven years Martin Biddle was to excavate alongside the cathedral. In that time he has uncovered the entire site of the Old Minster, and most complex it has proved to be. The walls above ground had been completely removed and to a great extent the foundations had also been dug out so that what remained was the earth-filled robber trenches indicating where the foundations had been. Biddle's task below ground was much the same as Dr Taylor's above ground; he had to work out from the fillings of the trenches and the way in which they overlapped each other, which stretches of foundation had belonged together, and which were earlier and which later. Fortunately, he was aided by good documentary evidence, which made it possible to identify the various parts of the church. Even then Biddle's excavations could produce at best a ground plan of the church, for there was nothing to indicate what the superstructure had looked like.

The sequence, once worked out, showed that the Minster was built around a church which measured some thirty metres long; this has been identified with reasonable certainty as the original church of Winchester built by King Cenwalh of Wessex in 648. Twenty metres to the west was an isolated rectangular building, probably the foundation of the tower of St Martin; and between the two, somewhere in the open, lay St Swithun's grave. The grave was

The chalk foundations of the building work carried out on the Old Minster between 971 and 974, seen from the roof of the cathedral.

subsequently enclosed by a building built on a massive chalk foundation which linked the main church to the tower; documents date this building to between 971 and 974. Finally in the last hundred years of the church's existence, this linking building was replaced by a massive square west end, the east end was extended with a lengthy apse, and projecting side chapels, apsidal and rectangular, were built on both sides of the church. The final plan shows a large, complicated and much altered building nearly seventy-six metres long.

Biddle's excavations have concentrated on exploring the church known as the Old Minster. This name dates from Saxon times; the church was called 'old' to distinguish it from the 'new' minster founded by Alfred. Alfred did not live to see the New Minster completed; it was not consecrated until 903. Now it too, like the Old Minster, has vanished completely. The New Minster is known to have been situated north of the Old Minster, and it was there, only a few steps away, that Martin Biddle found it. For the present this church is not being excavated, though one trench has been dug across it and parts of the south wall have been uncovered as a result of the work on the Old Minster. It was in the course of uncovering this wall that Biddle came across what must be his most spectacular find so far.

It is an ordinary block of stone which had been used in the foundations of the south wall of the New Minster; but before that it had been used in the wall of another building where it had been plastered and painted. By great good fortune the painted surface has survived almost undamaged. It shows the head and shoulders of a man with others behind him, part of a group of figures, alongside a decorative border. This block of stone shows only a small part of a scene, and we can never know what the rest of it was; but with the walls and even the floors of the two minsters swept away, this vivid fragment gives a glimpse of what these buildings must have been like inside.

The new material from excavations at places such as Winchester has provided a stimulus to renewed study of surviving buildings, and Dr Taylor has now combined with Martin Biddle to investigate again the problematical Anglo-Saxon church at Repton. Between them they are making a stone-by-stone examination of the existing walls, removing the blocking from former windows and doorways, and at the same time excavating alongside the church to study the foundations and the way in which the layers of soil have built up against them. It is in joint undertakings such as this that church archaeology will proceed in the future.

7

The Coming of
the Vikings

The Viking raids on England in the ninth century are described in great detail in the entries in the *Anglo-Saxon Chronicle*. Year after year the Danes landed and plundered the countryside before being driven off or leaving of their own accord. To begin with their raids were brief summer affairs, but in 851 they retreated only as far as the Isle of Thanet in east Kent and there they stayed for the winter. This was an ideal place from which to launch a raid up the Thames or anywhere around the coast. This was bad enough, but worse was to come. In 866, so the *Chronicle* records, 'a great heathen army came into England and took up winter quarters in East Anglia; and there they were supplied with horses, and the East Anglians made peace with them'. The Danes were now truly mobile across country and nowhere was safe from their attacks.

There is extremely telling evidence for the lightning effects of these Danish raids in the numbers of coins which were buried in hoards at this time. In the days before banks, burying one's savings was a way of keeping them safe; and there must always have been a large number of hoards buried in the ground. Normally the person who buried the coins would come back to recover them, but if he died without telling someone else where they were, then the coins were lost for ever. These are the hoards which are found occasionally today.

The numismatist Michael Dolley has made a study of the hoards of the Anglo-Saxon period found in England, and he has shown that for the decade 870–880 there are five times as many hoards of Anglo-Saxon coins found than is usual for any decade in the hundred years before or after. So dramatic an increase in the number of hoards is not recorded again till the years following 1066 and the Norman

Coins typical of those found in hoards buried between 870 and 880. Silver pennies of Burgred of Mercia and Alfred of Wessex.

Conquest. It is a clear indication of the insecurity of the times during the Viking raids.

The *Chronicle* carefully records where the Danish army spent the winter: Thanet in 865, East Anglia the following year, then York, Nottingham, York again, Thetford, Reading, London, Torksey, Repton and so on. At each of these places the Danes must have provided themselves with a safe retreat for the winter—an earthen bank and ditch, or a timber stockade, though no certain traces of any of these winter quarters has yet been found. Indeed, there is incredibly little evidence in the nature of actual objects to indicate the presence of the Danish army at all.

One of the few certain pieces of evidence comes from Reading. When gravel was being dug for the construction of the railway line alongside the River Thames in 1832 a Viking burial was found. Along with the skeleton of the man were found his sword and the skeleton of his horse. The sword is known to modern scholars from an old engraving made when it was first found, but its subsequent whereabouts were unknown till 1971 when it came to light again safely in the possession of the family who had first acquired it. The blade is now broken, and the lower half is missing; when found it was described as 'bent double', which corresponds with the common practice of 'killing' a sword, or rendering it useless, by folding it double in this way before putting it into a grave. The handgrip is protected by two brass crossguards inlaid with silver and copper wires and decorated with a variety of ornament which Viking archaeologists call 'gripping beast'. The sword dates from around 800, and must have been quite old when buried, for it is more than likely that the grave is that of one of the Vikings who was camped at Reading during the winter of 871–872 and who died perhaps of wounds received in the fierce fighting in which they were involved. The presence of the horse in the grave is a typical Viking custom; the practice of slaughtering horses to bury in graves is to be found wherever the Vikings went.

The north and east of England were rapidly overrun and dominated by the Danes, but they were unable to extinguish Alfred's resistance in the south-west. Eventually Alfred came to terms with Guthrum, the leader of the Danish army, and a treaty was signed between them dividing the country into two. This treaty document has survived and it is interesting to see that it begins by defining the boundary between Alfred's realm and Guthrum's realm. It reads: 'First there is the question of the boundary; it runs up the Thames [to London] and then up the River Lea, along the Lea to its source and

74

then in a straight line to Bedford, then up the River Ouse to Watling Street.'

The area to the north and east of this line came under Viking rule, and the laws of the Danes prevailed. As a result this part of England became known as the Danelaw. It is to be expected that there would be considerable evidence of the Viking presence in the Danelaw; but there is not. Here and there there are burials, such as the one found at Reading, and a few of these graves are women's graves, as one might expect in an area which became one of established settlement. But there are no extensive pagan cemeteries as there were for the early Anglo-Saxons. The total number of Viking

Brass fittings to the handle of the Viking sword from Reading.

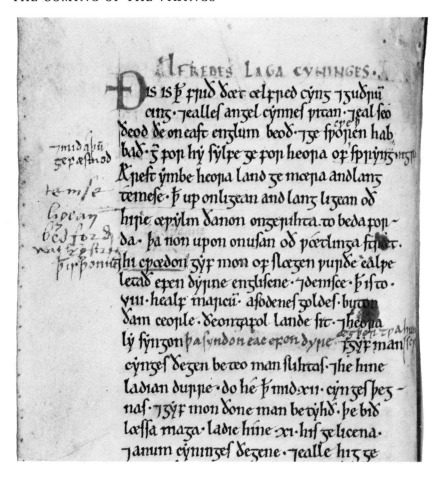

The document recording the treaty between Alfred and Guthrum. The boundary is described on lines five to eight of the main text.

graves from the whole of England amounts to no more than fourteen. How does this come to be so?

A most interesting explanation of this 'lack' of Viking graves has been put forward by Professor David Wilson, the Director of the British Museum. He has pointed to the fact that several of the few known Viking graves have been found in churchyards. They have been dug up by chance by gravediggers preparing new graves, and they have been recognised as Viking by the presence of some typical object, usually a weapon. The Danish settlers, so David Wilson suggests, mingled with the existing communities in England; and when they died they were buried in the traditional burial ground of the community, which was the village churchyard. They were buried with their weapons, so it would appear that they retained their pagan burial rites, yet there is no sign that this caused any problems; and the fact that there are so few of these graves implies that the Danes very quickly adopted a Christian belief.

This interesting suggestion is very neatly borne out by a stone cross found at Middleton near Pickering in Yorkshire. This is a normal wheel-headed cross, of which there are a great many in the north of England. It is carved with interlacing patterns and, on the shaft, on one side there is a dragon-like animal while on the other there is a figure of a Viking laid out in his grave. With him are his weapons, on one side his spear, on the other his sword and battle-axe; up above the left shoulder there is a round object which might be his shield, or his helmet seen from above, and in his right hand he holds a long knife

The two sides of the shaft of the Middleton cross.

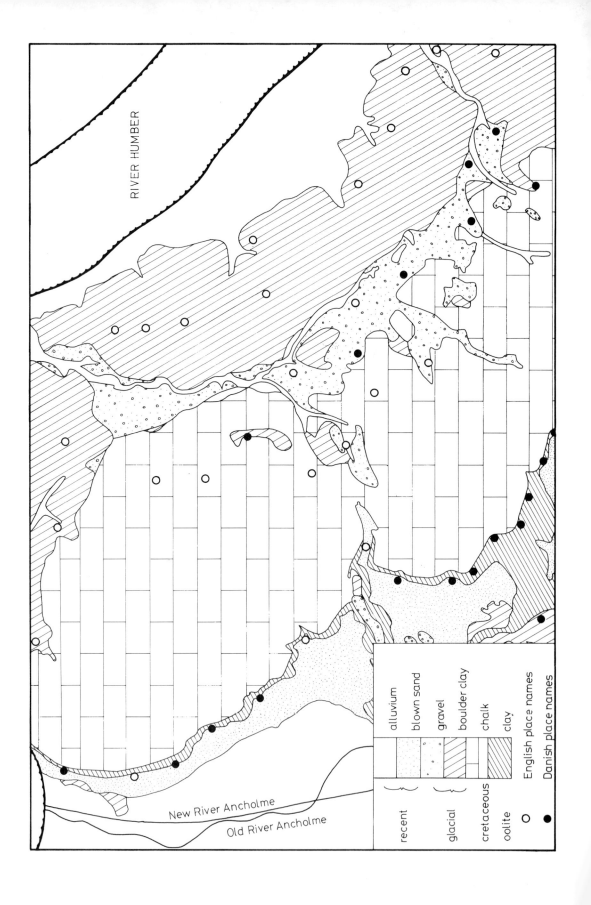

RIVER HUMBER

New River Ancholme

Old River Ancholme

			alluvium
recent			blown sand
			gravel
glacial			boulder clay
cretaceous			chalk
oolite			clay
	○	●	English place names / Danish place names

Geology and settlements in north-east Lincolnshire.

extending across his body at the level of his waist. The scene is exactly that of a pagan burial, and here it is represented on a Christian monument. There can be few more convincing examples of the adaptability of the beliefs of the Vikings to their new situation.

The Scandinavian *Egil's Saga*, written in the thirteenth century, has an interesting comment on the beliefs and practices of the Vikings who first settled in England. 'It was a common custom,' it says, 'both among merchants and those mercenaries who joined with the Christians, to be provisionally baptised, since men who received provisional baptism had full contact with Christians and heathens, but kept whatever faith they were inclined to.' No doubt there was a good deal of aiming for the best of both worlds.

The Viking burials which have been found are pitifully few and in no way come near to justifying the description which the *Chronicle* gives us of the Vikings 'sharing' out the land and 'cultivating it'. However we know for certain that they did do this, and the evidence comes not from any excavation but from the land itself, from the villages and towns which exist today, and from the names by which we know them. Derby and Grimsby, Kirby and Kirkby, Flixborough and Ferrybridge, Thurmaston, Ravensthorpe, Micklethwaite and Ulleskelf—all are Scandinavian names, and when a map of England is drawn and each Scandinavian village name is marked with a spot we are provided with a most dramatic illustration of the reality of the Viking settlements. Northern and eastern England are covered with a mass of dots while southern England and the south-west Midlands are completely bare. If the line of the boundary agreed in the treaty between Alfred and Guthrum is also put on the map one can see that this corresponds very closely with the division of the country as indicated by the Scandinavian place-names.

The Danish army was called 'The Great Army' but even so it was to be numbered in hundreds rather than thousands, and it is inconceivable that there were enough Vikings in it to account for all the places which have Scandinavian names. The number and extent of these places suggest the presence of many thousands of settlers in northern and eastern England, and it seems clear that the initial 'sharing out of the land' must have been followed by a steady flow of new immigrants from Denmark. When looked at in detail the evidence of the place-names shows in a most revealing way where these new immigrants settled.

To see how this works it is best to understand a little more about place-names and the way in which they were formed. The familiar

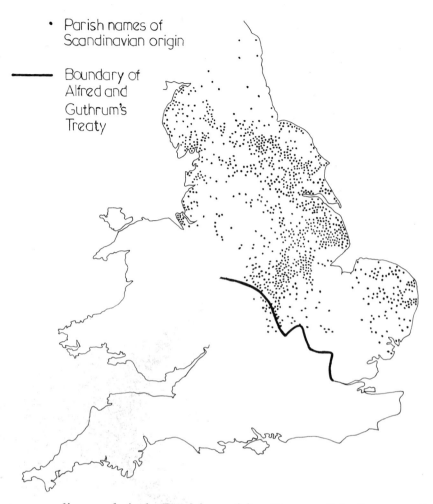

Scandinavian place names showing the extent of Viking settlement.

name-ending . . . *by* is the Danish word for village, and the first part of the name is either a personal name, the name of the founder of the village, or a word which described some particular feature of the village. Thus Grimsby is 'Grimr's village', and Kirkby is the 'church village' or the 'village with a church', and so on. Sometimes the names which have survived in use are a mixture of Danish and English, so-called hybrid names. Grimston is an example of this, the final syllable . . . *ton* is the English word for village, so Grimston also means 'Grimr's village' though in this case it is a hybrid of a Danish personal name and an English word.

In the last few years the relationship between the Scandinavian place-names and the actual villages themselves has been the subject of special study by Professor Kenneth Cameron of Nottingham University. He has been involved in lengthy and painstaking research into the type of land which each village occupies; is it best-quality

agricultural land and is the soil well drained? Or is it a heavy clay soil, or a poor thin soil that would not have been worth cultivating? Professor Cameron's research has involved a detailed study of the land that might be thought to have nothing to do with the Viking settlements, but he has shown that it has. He has concentrated on the area of the north-east Midlands which belonged to the Five Boroughs, Derby, Nottingham, Leicester, Lincoln and Stamford. This area had been occupied and settled by Anglian people in the fifth and sixth centuries and their villages were in existence when the Vikings arrived. The Anglian settlers had had the pick of the countryside, and it is not surprising that their villages occupied the best land. Professor Cameron's work has shown that many of the hybrid names, the 'Grimstons', are villages which occupy sites which are just as good as those occupied by the Anglian villages. In many cases villages with Anglian, or English, names and those with hybrid names are side by side on land which is equally good. A good example of this is to be seen in the villages around Leicester. The hybrid names Thurmaston and Thrussington are situated on the well-drained gravel soils of the valleys of the River Wreak and the Soar in exactly the same sort of positions as are the English named villages Belgrave, Birstall, Wanlip and Syston which surround them. From this evidence Professor Cameron suggests that the hybrid names are places which were originally English villages but which were taken over by a Viking or group of Vikings at the time of the 'sharing out of the land' and that the name was changed as a result.

However, yet more striking is his discovery that the names which are entirely Scandinavian, those which have the ending . . . *by* and others like them, are situated on land which is less good than the hybrid and English names. Professor Cameron suggests that these villages were new settlements made at a time when the best land was already occupied. Anyone familiar with the north-east Midlands or with Yorkshire will know that these . . . *by* names are very common and it is easy to see that there must have been extensive areas of the country where new settlers moved in and built their villages. The scale of this new settlement can be seen by the very common occurrence of Danish named villages on the Lincolnshire Wolds. Towards the coast there is a line of English named villages, from Barrow-on-Humber down to Great Coates, which are situated on a chalky boulder clay type of soil which is easily worked and produces good crops. Further inland there is a line of Danish named villages situated on the much less desirable gravel which has a much less

Above
An enamelled escutcheon with millefiori glass insets from the large Sutton Hoo hanging bowl.

Below
A painted block of stone, once part of a wall painting, which was reused in building the foundations of the New Minster at Winchester about AD 903.

81

A pair of tortoise brooches from a Viking woman's grave at Santon Downham, Norfolk. The pair of brooches indicates a style of dress which had gone out of fashion among Anglo-Saxon women three hundred years before.

fertile soil and is so badly drained that it is often marshy. On the western edge of the Wolds there is another line of Danish named villages on sites which were not sufficiently good to attract the English three hundred years before. The story which emerges from Professor Cameron's study is that the hybrid names, and there are comparatively few of them, indicate villages which the Vikings took over from the English; and the far more common Danish named places such as the . . . *by* names suggest extensive and continuous settlement of less good land by new arrivals from overseas. It is as though large numbers of people were encouraged to come and farm those areas which had not previously been occupied. Professor Cameron's study, combining geology and geography with his own special skills in language, has provided a full answer where no archaeological excavation could have done so.

While the Scandinavian settlement is a very well documented fact, it receives little support from the sort of archaeological evidence that can be dug up. The Middleton cross shows why this is so; the newcomers blended quickly into the landscape, fulfilling a role as farmers alongside the well-established English settlers. The scattered evidence of the place-names, once interpreted as it has been, shows just how important and extensive this settlement was.

So far we have considered the north-eastern part of the country, but the north-west, Cumbria and Lancashire and Cheshire, have their Scandinavian names too. Some of these names are derived from specifically Norwegian words as opposed to Danish words, and they indicate that the settlers on this western coast must have been Norwegian rather than Danish Vikings. The Norwegian Vikings had raided and occupied Ireland and the Isle of Man in much the same way as the Danish Vikings had raided England; their settlements on the north-west coast of England are hardly referred to in the written sources, but their raids from Ireland have left behind the largest silver treasure ever to be found in England.

This treasure was found at Cuerdale in Lancashire in 1840. It had been buried in a lead-lined chest about forty metres from the bank of the River Ribble just about where the M6 motorway now crosses it to the east of Preston. The chest contained a thousand ounces of scrap silver and over seven thousand silver coins. The coins were mostly English and Danish but they also included Continental silver coins, coins from the Byzantine Empire, and Islamic coins from the Arab world in the east. The scrap silver included pieces of English and Irish objects cut up and kept purely for their bullion value; many had already been melted down and cast into small silver ingots. The coins can be used to date this treasure to about 906.

Many Vikings, as we have seen, came and settled in England; others seem always to have been more interested in the loot which they could collect or the tribute they could exact to make them go away. In this they were remarkably successful—with the result that there are now more Anglo-Saxon coins in the museums of Scandinavia than there are in English museums. The Cuerdale hoard is probably a typical hoard of loot from a successful expedition, but in this case the Vikings to whom it belonged failed to get away with it.

Ingots and scrap silver from the Cuerdale hoard.

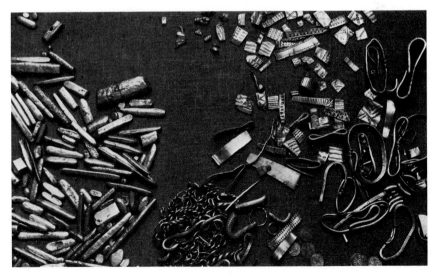

8

The Growth of the Towns

Excavation in towns is a difficult business. Much as they might like to, archaeologists obviously cannot dig where they please. Their chance comes when old buildings are being pulled down and sites are being prepared for redevelopment. The archaeologist must then negotiate with the development company and with the builders for permission to dig. Often it happens that the areas available are severely restricted by the position of the foundations of the new buildings, and the result of the excavation is likely to be fragmentary—a bit of a building here, a few rubbish pits there—and all cut into and partly destroyed by the cellars and rubbish pits of their successors. It is not surprising that the results of any one individual excavation inside a town are often inconclusive. It is only when the pieces are brought together that the jigsaw begins to take shape and a pattern emerges.

One of the jigsaws where the pattern is beginning to show is Winchester. Excavating the Old Minster has been only a part of Martin Biddle's job; his prime concern has been to discover the history of Winchester at all stages of its growth, how it was founded and how it has developed through the ages. This has involved excavations in all parts of the town. Biddle has found that Winchester began as a Roman town; it was the capital of the tribal area of the Belgae who inhabited that part of Britain and it was called *Venta Belgarum*, Venta of the Belgae. The Roman town covered a roughly rectangular area; it was surrounded by a wall and was laid out inside with a criss-cross grid of streets in proper Roman fashion. There were gates on each side leading out to the surrounding countryside.

These walls and gateways have provided the framework for the subsequent history of Winchester, but the Roman street pattern has

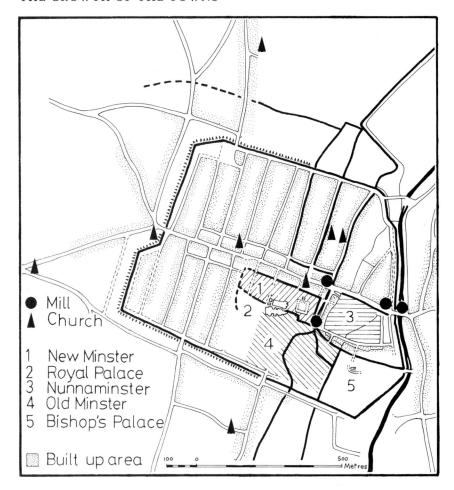

Mill

Church

1 New Minster
2 Royal Palace
3 Nunnaminster
4 Old Minster
5 Bishop's Palace

Built up area

100   0   500
                               Metres

Winchester in late
Saxon times.

disappeared completely. As a result of his excavations Martin Biddle
has been able to trace the present-day streets back through the Middle
Ages to late Saxon times, and he has found that at that time too they
formed a remarkably regular subdivision of the area within the walls.
This arrangement was as regular in its own way as the Roman one, but
it was different. The main street of the late Saxon town was
appropriately the High Street which runs roughly east–west between
two of the main gates. A Roman road had followed the same route, but
it had been on a distinctly different alignment. Parallel to the High
Street and some twenty-seven metres from it on either side were
secondary streets which served to give access to the backs of the
properties along the High Street. These three streets formed the
backbone of the town. The rest of the area was divided up by streets
running out at right angles from the High Street to the walls where
they met another street which ran round inside the walls.

85

Biddle has argued that this rearrangement of the streets within the walls of Winchester is too regular to be due to chance; it must be due to a deliberate decision made by the 'powers that be'. He has accumulated various sorts of evidence to show when this plan came into being. In the first place he has excavated parts of two streets which were blocked by the building of the Norman castle in 1067. Although this excavation produced no dating evidence, it was found that the streets had been laid down and resurfaced as many as seven times before they were buried. Clearly they must have been built many years before the Norman Conquest. Useful dating evidence came from a trench across the modern Trafalgar Street, which in the Middle Ages had been known as *Gerestret*. Here too a succession of street surfaces was found, and lying on top of the lowest surface was a coin of Edward the Elder who died in 925. Further evidence comes indirectly from written sources. Biddle has pointed to a charter—a record of a transfer of property—which describes the boundaries of a certain property with reference to the streets of Winchester. This document is dated 904, so the new layout must be earlier than that.

Martin Biddle has extended the ideas which have come from his Winchester excavations to other towns. Working in collaboration with an historian, David Hill, he has shown how other Saxon towns seem to have been laid out in a regular fashion. Good examples where the street system is known are Wareham in Dorset and Wallingford in Oxfordshire. Though much smaller than Winchester, both these towns seem to have been laid out in the same way, and since they are not old Roman towns, this involved the building of their surrounding walls and ramparts too. It seems very much as though all these places were either reinstated or built from new as part of a single overall plan at some time in the ninth century.

This idea links up very neatly with a document known as the *Burghal Hidage*. This document gives a list of the towns of Alfred's day which were provided with fortified defences against the Danish Vikings. A 'burh' was a fortified town, and a 'hide' was a unit of agricultural land; the 'hidage' for each burh was the amount of land required to provide men to defend the town in case of emergency. The document gives a formula for working this out. A hide was roughly the amount of land which a family would need to support itself, and each hide of land had to contribute one man for the maintenance and defence of the town. Four men were required for each pole's length of wall, which, since a pole is five and a half yards, meant that each man had to defend a length of wall equal to $4\frac{1}{8}$ feet. Thus knowing the number of hides required for each town it is possible to work out the length of the walls at that time.

Winchester is rated at 2,400 hides, which is equivalent to 2,400 men for maintenance and defence. At $4\frac{1}{8}$ feet per man, this makes the length of the walls equal to 9,900 feet. The length of the walls at Winchester as revealed by the excavations is 9,954 feet, which is a very impressive demonstration of the accuracy of the figures in the *Burghal Hidage*. At some other towns, Exeter and Oxford for example, the lines of the Saxon defences are not yet known for certain, and the figures given by the *Burghal Hidage* can be used to suggest where they might be.

The *Burghal Hidage* describes that part of England which Alfred defended, and its northern boundary with the exception of Buckingham is the Thames. But after Alfred's death, in the years of his sons and daughter, there was a gradual Saxon reconquest of the Midlands, and more defended burhs were constructed there on the same principle as in the south. One of these sites which has been particularly well explored is Tamworth. It was built, so the *Chronicle*

Superimposed surfaces of a late Saxon street sealed below the earthworks of the Norman castle at Winchester.

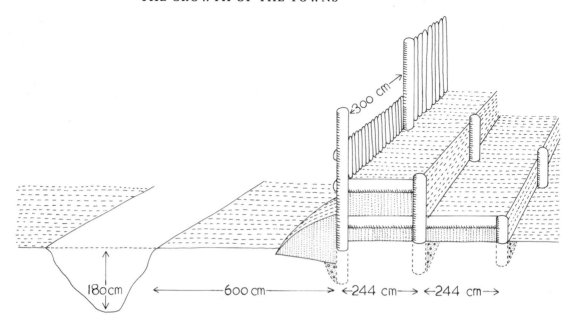

300 cm

180cm ← 600 cm → ← 244 cm → ← 244 cm →

Reconstruction showing the turf and timber defences on the west side of Tamworth.

tells us, in the early summer of 913, and the builder was Alfred's daughter, Aethelflaed, known as the 'Lady of the Mercians'.

Since 1960 there have been five different sets of excavations at Tamworth, and each has added a little more to our knowledge of the early history of the place. Now the line of Aethelflaed's defences is known on three sides, the west, north and east, while the south is formed by the rivers Anker and Tame. The most revealing of these excavations have been those carried out in 1967 and 1968 by the local archaeologist Jim Gould. He has uncovered the remains of the west gate of Saxon Tamworth and a stretch of the wall nearby. The 'wall' itself was a bank of earth forming a rampart 4.9 metres wide; this was held in place by stout timbers, long since rotted away, but clearly indicated by their post holes, which were found regularly spaced throughout the bank. Along the outer edge of the bank were traces of smaller timbers between the large ones as though the bank had been fronted with timber and crowned with a wooden palisade. But none of this can be certain, for the turf stack of which the bank was made only survived to a height of thirty centimetres. In front of the wall was a level space, the berm, which was six metres wide, and beyond that a ditch 3.6 metres wide and 1.8 metres deep. The west gate was found just beside the present Lichfield Road. The bank was much wider at the actual gateway and was heavily interlaced with timbers throughout. These timbers included two rows of very massive posts which Jim Gould suggests were probably the supports for a bridge or walkway across the top of the gate. The road through the gate, Lichfield Road, has been in constant use for the past 1,000 years, and the ground has been so worn away that the present street level is now almost a metre lower than the remains of Aethelflaed's gate.

One curious detail of the excavations at Tamworth has been that at several places around the wall traces of an earlier earthwork have been discovered. In places parts of a ditch have been found, in others parts of a bank. It looks as though there was some sort of defence work here before Aethelflaed built her fort. Other early defence works—that is earlier than the planned towns of Alfred's day—have recently been discovered at Hereford and it is beginning to look very much as though settlements were being fortified earlier in the Midlands than in the south of England, where so many have survived. It is interesting to note that the earliest mention of towns being fortified is given in a document referring to the Midlands. The document refers to the 'construction of bridges and the building of defences' as being two duties which everyone was expected to take part in when the need arose. This document was issued in 749, so it seems certain that some towns were being enclosed as early as that.

There is as yet no clue to the date of the earlier defences at Tamworth, though they may well date from the end of the eighth century, for at that time there was a mill there. The finding of this is a spectacular and unique event, due to the fortunate fact that the

Philip Rahtz's reconstruction of the mill at Tamworth.

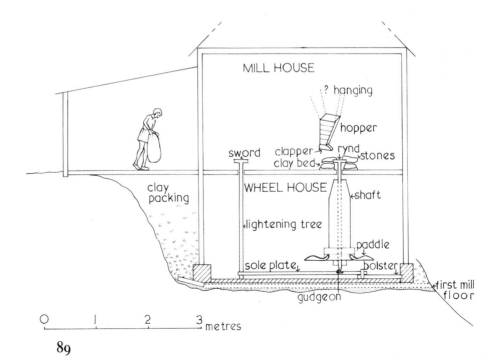

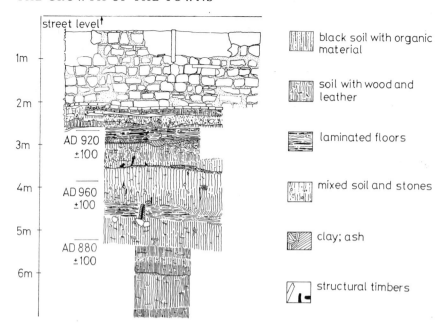

street level

1m

2m

3m AD 920
    ±100

4m AD 960
    ±100

5m AD 880
    ±100

6m

black soil with organic material

soil with wood and leather

laminated floors

mixed soil and stones

clay; ash

structural timbers

Cross-section of the deposits excavated below the new Lloyd's Bank Building in Pavement, York. The dates are calculated from radiocarbon measurements on waterlogged timber.

ground was waterlogged and the lower timbers of the mill had been preserved. The superstructure had disappeared and the surviving remains had been cut into by later features, including a well which had dug right through them, but this did not destroy the evidence of the mill. The millpond, the water channels, the framework of the mill house and, all important, fragments of millstones have survived to show what the building was. The millwheel seems to have been set up horizontally with the millstone at the upper end of its shaft so that the two rotated together without the need of any gearing. The millstone was about sixty centimetres in diameter. Water from the millpond was directed onto the blades of the millwheel causing it to turn. Speed could be controlled by adjusting the flow of water by means of a sluice gate, and if the mill was not needed, surplus water from the millpond could be let out through a second sluice.

One of the most interesting finds from this excavation is an unspectacular lump of material, a baulk of wood with a piece of iron embedded in it. In the centre of the iron there is a hollow which shows clear signs of having been worn smooth by something rotating in it. There seems little doubt that this is one of the bearings for the shaft which carried the millwheel and the millstone. It is an insignificant looking object, but one without which the mill could not have worked. The date of the mill has been established by using the radiocarbon method on the timbers which have survived, and gives a date in the range of 700–770.

The Viking areas of England had their towns too, though the archaeological evidence for them has not been so forthcoming as it has been for the English towns in the south. Archaeologists in these towns are now concentrating on finding out more about their early history, and it is likely that the next few years will produce some interesting results. However, in one Viking town, the story has already started to come to life; that town is York, or Jorvik as the Vikings called it.

In York, as in Winchester, the Roman defences have provided a framework for later developments, but it is a framework that has been used in quite a different way. In Saxon or Viking times the Roman legionary fortress situated in the angle between the River Ouse and its tributary the River Foss was linked to the two rivers by additional fortifications. This created an extensive enclosure on the north-east side of the Ouse matching that of the old Roman civilian settlement on the opposite bank. It was within these areas that the people lived, worked and traded.

In this enclosure the waterlogged nature of the low-lying land alongside the river has preserved not merely a single layer of timber foundations but layer upon layer of them amounting to a total deposit several metres thick. These deposits have recently been examined by Peter Addyman, the director of the York Archaeological Trust, in what must be one of the most extraordinary excavations ever undertaken.

Addyman's site was inside a standing building—a building which has now been converted into a branch of Lloyds Bank in the street known as Pavement. Before the bank started digging out vaults and reconstructing the inside of the building, Addyman moved into the cellars, lifted the floors and began digging downwards.

The area available in each cellar was very small, and there was never hope of getting anything like the complete plan of a building; a few square metres was all that was possible. Nevertheless the excavation continued downwards for more than five metres without coming to the bottom of the waterlogged deposits.

The 'soil' beneath the cellar floors was composed of alternate layers of fine clay and dark soil full of organic remains—all the sorts of things which have normally rotted away, and which only survive when the ground is waterlogged.

The remains of buildings appeared as the timbers and wattlework of the walls, and planks and brushwood from the floors. Wherever there was any trace of a wall it was found to run parallel to the present boundaries of the houses above, either along the street or at right

Enlarged view of insects—*Aglenus brunneus* and *Crypto-pleurum minutum*—typical of many species which occur in rotting organic debris, found in waterlogged deposits below the new branch of Lloyd's Bank in Pavement, York.

Antler comb from
recent excavations in
the Coppergate, York.

angles to it. This shows that the direction of these boundaries has not changed through all the years since the first timber buildings were placed here, and one may assume that the line of the street today is much the same as it was in the beginning.

Everywhere in and around the remains of the houses was debris which indicated what they had been used for. Much of this debris was connected with leather and leather industries; scraps of leather, offcuts from the cobbler's trade, were abundant. Along with the timber and leather the waterlogged conditions had preserved the remains of plants and insects. Addyman's diggers found thousands and thousands of the puparia of the common housefly and the stable fly, and of the scarabeid beetle and other insects, and these have been interpreted as the remains of the scavengers who fed on the waste products which were scraped from the animal skins in the process of preparing them for tanning. There was also a lot of chicken debris; feathers, eggshell fragments, and the remains of a beetle that lives in chicken houses. It seems that the chickens either lived in the houses, or that all these products of the hen house were brought in with chicken dung which was used in the leather tanning process. It is difficult to believe that anyone can actually have been living in these buildings, but even as workshops they must have been indescribably squalid, with piles of dung and fly-infested animal skins about the place; the smell is hard to imagine. Apart from these bizarre finds the waterlogged conditions have preserved ordinary objects such as wooden tools and bowls and platters, all types of object which have so often rotted away.

The deposits under the Lloyds Bank vaults range in date from the ninth to the twelfth century, and below them there are earlier deposits which have yet to be explored. The extraordinary finds from this very small area whet the appetite for what a full-scale excavation of a large site in this part of York will produce. Such a site has recently become available in the Coppergate and is now being excavated.

Leather shoe from the
Coppergate, York.

9

When the digging is done...

Who would think of making an X-ray of an iron buckle? No one did, until the 1950s. Now it is standard practice for most of the iron objects found in excavations to be X-rayed.

This has happened largely as a result of the research of Miss Vera Evison, a lecturer in Anglo-Saxon Archaeology at Birkbeck College, London. Early in the 1950s she was studying a particular type of early Anglo-Saxon ironwork which is decorated with strips of other metals set into grooves cut in the surface of the iron. The inlaid metal was usually brass or copper; sometimes both were used, and when polished they provided a bright and striking contrast with the iron. The objects favoured for this treatment were small pieces such as buckles and firesteels. On some of the best preserved the decoration showed up clearly, but Miss Evison soon realised that many likely-looking pieces were covered with layers of rust and it was impossible to say whether there was any inlay on them or not. Old finds from excavations in the last century were now so dry and brittle that it was impossible to clean off the rust, and only X-rays could show whether there was anything beneath the dirt. Miss Evison embarked on a programme of X-raying these iron objects, and her results were startling. Many pieces which had lain in museums for years, and had never been thought of as anything more than uninteresting lumps of iron, came to life under the X-ray, and an unexpectedly large number of inlaid objects was discovered.

Following the use of X-raying for this specific project, it was soon realised that the technique was of more widespread general application, for not only did the X-rays show up the inlaying of different sorts of metal, but they also showed up the original shape of

Pattern-welded sword blade, found near Ely.

the iron objects; lumps of iron which had been shapeless and unrecognisable now became identifiable for what they were. The reason for this is simple. The X-rays penetrate the lump of iron and pass through it to record an image on a sensitive photographic plate behind it. Metals like brass and copper resist the passage of the X-rays more than iron does, so the X-rays have less effect on the film under the inlay than they do under the plain iron; similarly the iron resists the X-rays more than the layers of rust and dirt, so the actual outline of the object shows up differently from the overall outline of the corroded lump. This is so useful an aid to cleaning objects after they have been excavated that it is now standard practice to X-ray iron objects before attempting to remove any of the corrosion from them.

There is, of course, unlikely to be any mistake in identifying a sword, but swords are also X-rayed and this shows whether or not the blade is pattern-welded. Pattern-welding is the name used to describe a particular technique for making sword blades; it is derived from the fact that the finished blades appear to be decorated with most elaborate spiral and zigzag patterns. These patterns show up as a difference in colouring, alternate bands of light and dark, on the surface of the iron blade. Sometimes when the blade has survived in good condition, as often happens when it has been lost in a river, the pattern still shows up clearly today; but more often the pattern is covered by the corrosion, and is only revealed by X-raying the blade.

A pattern-welded sword blade found near Ely in Cambridgeshire was examined in detail by Herbert Maryon, a former director of the British Museum's Research Laboratory. The patterning was confined to two broad strips running down the faces of the blade; the remainder, the edges and the core, were plain. Maryon found that the light and dark bands of the pattern had different compositions; the bright silvery metal was steel, the darker metal iron.

Maryon thought that the blade was made up of bars of metal composed of thin strips of iron and thin strips of steel, but he was unable to reproduce a blade in this way, and it now seems likely that the result occurred almost by accident.

When wrought iron is heated in a charcoal fire it absorbs a small amount of carbon with the result that the surface of the iron is converted to steel. The process of working the iron involves the repeated hammering out of the heated metal, then folding it and heating and hammering again. The folding brings the steel surfaces together, and makes a sandwich of steel between wrought iron. Repeated folding and hammering creates a finely laminated structure of layers of wrought iron interspersed with steel. This structure was ideal for a weapon blade for it combined the hardness of steel with the resilience of wrought iron.

Normally the laminated structure of the iron would not show on the surface of a blade, but it could be made to show—as Maryon demonstrated—by twisting. When a narrow rod of the laminated metal is heated, the laminations are set on edge, and when the surface is ground smooth, the contrast between the steel and the iron becomes visible.

The pattern on the Ely blade was formed by welding four narrow rods of twisted metal side by side on the face of the blade. The rods were arranged with twists alternately to left and right and the resulting pattern has a herring-bone appearance. Other patterns, spirals and zigzags, could be produced from the same twisted rods by grinding away more metal and cutting deeper into the twist.

Firesteel from High-down, Sussex, grave 14. Above, as it is; below, with the decorative inlay revealed by X-ray.

X-raying has shown that pattern-welding was widespread in Anglo-Saxon times, and there is little doubt that phrases such as 'patterned like serpents' and 'ring-patterned' by which the Anglo-Saxons described their blades must refer to pattern-welding. From a functional point of view pattern-welding served to show that the blade was a well-worked one of high quality; but that was all, for the twisting added no strength to the metal, and pattern-welded blades were no stronger than others made of well-worked iron.

95

Scientific testing of another sort has recently been used to establish the date of the royal burial mound at Sutton Hoo and thus the identity of the king buried there. This has involved the analysis of the coins from the burial—a project whose success is due to the fruitful co-operation between the numismatist John Kent and the scientist Andrew Oddy.

Archaeologists usually look to coins—if they are lucky enough to have found any—to provide them with an accurate date but, as we saw earlier, the coins found in the Sutton Hoo barrow could not be dated by conventional means. There were no coins being minted in England at that time, and the thirty-seven coins in the burial are all from France, from the Merovingian dynasties. It is a characteristic of many Merovingian coins that, although they carry the name of the place where they were minted, few bear a king's name; so it is difficult to date them at all accurately. However there is another way. In the sixth century Merovingian coins were made of gold—tiny pieces weighing about 1.2 grams each—but from the end of the sixth century onwards the shortage of gold caused the coinage to be debased by the addition of silver. As the seventh century proceeded the proportion of silver was increased so that by the end of the century the coinage had become a silver one. Kent and Oddy realised that if they could find out how the debasement had proceeded they would have established a sort of time scale; they would then only have to calculate the proportions of gold and silver in any coin to find out roughly when it had been minted.

The first problem was to find a satisfactory method of analysis of the coins, for they must not be damaged in any way, and there was no question of breaking off pieces or drilling out samples for testing. Andrew Oddy developed a method of analysis by specific gravity. The density of pure gold is known, and so is the density of pure silver; the density of alloys with various proportions of each metal could thus be calculated. Once this was done, it was then simply a job of calculating the density of each of the coins and seeing how this related to the known percentages. The density of the coins was calculated by carefully weighing each coin twice, once normally in air and the second time suspended in a liquid whose properties were known. Oddy's method had to be foolproof, and a lot of trouble was taken finding the most suitable liquid and taking precautions against errors, but once perfected he went to France to weigh the coins in museums there. At this stage he was concentrating on those coins which were dated by a king's name or perhaps that of a bishop. In all Oddy

UR:CASTELLVM:AT:HESTENGA:CEASTRA — HIC:NVNTIATVM:EST:WILLELM:DE:HAROLD: — hIC

VVILLELMI:DVCIS:PVGNANT:CONTRA:DINANTES:ET:

VT:CIBVM:RAPERENTVR: — HIC:EST:VVADARD:

Above
The Bayeux Tapestry:
Saxon peasants build
William's castle at
Hastings.

Middle
The Bayeux Tapestry:
the central tower and
timber palisade of the
castle at Dinan.

Below
Deserted timber
houses representing a
village being plun-
dered by the Norman
knight Wadard, and
his foraging party, who
lead away the live-
stock.

weighed some 900 dated Merovingian coins, and for each of these he calculated the density and thus the proportion of gold and silver. From these results John Kent was able to prepare a chart showing how the debasement had taken place. As perhaps we might have expected, it was not a straightforward gradual change, but a series of downward steps indicating how, as the supply of gold became exhausted, the quality of the coinage had to be reduced.

Once the progress of the debasement had been worked out in this way it was a straightforward matter to use the chart to estimate the date of the other coins. The same weighing measurements gave a value for the density and thus for the gold/silver content of each coin; and, knowing this, the date could be read off from the chart.

The Sutton Hoo coins had gold contents which varied from 98% down to 67%, suggesting dates over a period of fifty years before and after AD 600. The latest coins are the ones which give the date of the group which John Kent has estimated was collected together between about AD 615 and 625. This very neat analytical solution to a difficult yet crucial question provides a degree of certainty which stylistic and artistic methods of dating can never hope to do.

Cemeteries, as we have seen, can provide a host of objects to throw light on the behaviour and customs of those buried in them but, unless they are situated on acid sandy soil like Sutton Hoo, they also provide skeletons and these give us details that no amount of jewellery possibly could. Most obvious are the monstrous deformities and severe injuries resulting from disease, accident or warfare. Examples are not rare. A woman at Alfriston in Sussex had a tubercular infection of the left hip which caused her left thigh to fuse solid in its joint, yet she managed to hobble around, who knows how, for many years. A young man from Thetford in Norfolk suffered a compound fracture, breaking both the bones in his left leg. His contracting muscles caused the broken ends to overlap and without proper setting they eventually healed in this way leaving him with a sound leg, but one which was an inch shorter than the other. A man from Thorpe St Catherine, Norfolk, has a gash in his skull caused by a sharp weapon such as a sword or an axe. The blade bit deeply into the skull and a large piece of bone was broken away; there is no sign of any healing — the man must have died at once.

These spectacular abnormalities show up readily even to those with little experience of examining skeletons, and it is this sort of thing which has always attracted attention in the past as it still does today. But now it is normal practice for excavators to have each skeleton

Healed fractures in the left leg of a man from Thetford, Norfolk.

Andrew Oddy weighing coins in the British Museum Research Laboratory.

carefully examined by someone who is an expert on bones, and all sorts of less obvious details are being discovered. Some of the most exciting and absorbing discoveries of recent years have been made by Calvin Wells, who was himself once a practising surgeon but has for many years now been concerned as an anthropologist in the study of bones from excavated cemetcries. Recently he has demonstrated the existence of a highly skilled surgeon who performed trephinations in East Anglia in the later sixth century.

Trephination is the operation of cutting a hole in the skull and exposing the brain within. It has been performed at various times since the Neolithic period, though it was clearly more popular among some people than others. Greek, Roman and Arab doctors have recorded details of the reasons for the operation: it is clear that it was designed to treat disease or injury, and perhaps nervous disorders such as epilepsy and madness. When successful the wound would heal without infection; when unsuccessful the patient would die.

Calvin Wells has now recognised six cases of skulls with holes from trephination operations. Holes in the skull are not all that uncommon, and can be due to a number of causes. When Calvin Wells came across the first of the six examples he was careful to point out that the hole could be the result of a healed wound, and need not be due to trephination; so too with his second example. But recent excavations have produced four more examples, all from the same area of East Anglia, all of about the same date, and all with the same characteristic holes; and Calvin Wells has had to reconsider his earlier statements. The holes are all shaped like long oval grooves cut in the skull so that they expose a small area of the brain. The grooves seem to have been cut with a tool like a gouge which has gradually pared away the bone until it has made a hole. The shapes of these holes are the same, the sizes are the same and even the angles of slope of the sides of the holes

Healed trephination in the skull of a man from Swaffham.

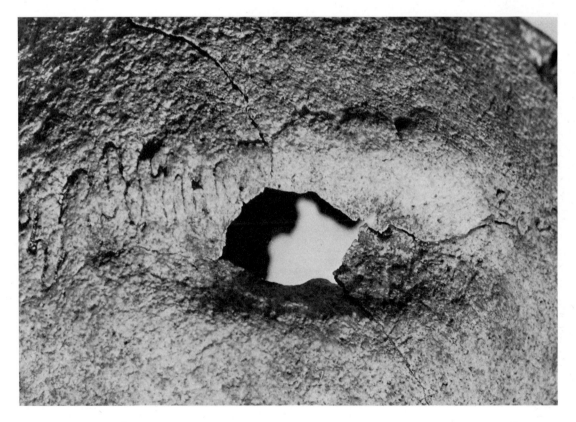

Potsherds from Sutton Courtenay showing the holes of burnt-out grass-tempering.

are the same; the similarity is such that Calvin Wells suggests that the operations were performed not merely by the same technique, but by the same man!

We cannot know how he came by his skill, nor really why he chose to operate in this way, nor whether the ailments he was treating were alleviated. We are left merely with his handiwork—the skulls of his patients—but what is remarkable about these is that all show that the wounds healed with the minimum of infection. In the primitive conditions of the day there could be no greater tribute to the skill of this long forgotten master surgeon.

The effects of primitive trephination operations—on the patient and on the surgeon—can never be known, for no one is going to repeat such an operation today by way of an experiment. But, in fields where experiments are possible, we can often learn a great deal by attempting to repeat ancient procedures. We may not know whether we have got the procedure right, but the experience can be instructive, as I have discovered for myself.

Much of the pottery from early Anglo-Saxon sites is what archaeologists call 'grass-tempered'. The name comes from the texture of the pottery which is made from clay mixed with some vegetable matter like grass. When fired the grass burns out leaving hollows in the surface of the pot. These burnt out hollows are never very large, and they show that if the material added really was grass then the pieces must have been chopped up very small. The question then arises: Why? Is it really grass? What purpose does it serve?

By chance one day I came across an account of the same sort of pottery in Holland in which the author suggested that the material added to the clay was not grass but horse dung. If this were so it would explain why the burnt out hollows were small, for once chewed and digested by a horse, no piece of grass is very large. The suggestion seemed a good one; but what would happen in practice? It seemed a case for a trial.

I approached the first stage—the mixing of the clay and the dung—with some reticence! The clay which I was using was not a good clay for working by hand; it was crumbly and could only with difficulty be made to hold together to make a small pot. But the mixture of clay and dung, once kneaded thoroughly together, turned out to be an excellent material for working by hand. It was soft and tenacious without being sticky and could be built up into a pot-shape quite freely in the hand. The walls could be made very thin and still keep their shape, and as the surface of the pot began to dry it could be burnished almost to a shine. When these pots were fired in a bonfire, the grass material in the dung burned out leaving hollows very like those on Anglo-Saxon pottery.

The result shows that a most unsuitable crumbly clay could be converted into a very suitable potting medium simply by the addition of a liberal proportion of horse dung. An improbable explanation perhaps—but a simple one that has all the appearances of being correct.

10

The Coming of the Normans

The Anglo-Saxon age was brought to an end by the Norman Conquest. There is no doubt of that. The story of that fateful year 1066 is well recorded by English and by Norman writers, as well as being vividly portrayed in pictures in the Bayeux Tapestry.

William of Poitiers, a Norman who wrote an account of the Conquest soon after it happened, tells us that when William came to England he landed at Pevensey and he built a castle there. He then moved to Hastings and built another castle and it was from this castle that he set out to fight against Harold. The building of the castle at Hastings is shown in the Bayeux Tapestry. Men are at work digging and shovelling soil up on to a mound; around the top of the mound there is some kind of timber stockade. The scene is carefully identified in the Latin inscription which is embroidered into the tapestry: '*iussit ut foderetur castellum at Hestinga ceastra*', 'he ordered that a castle be built at Hastings'.

A castle exactly like the Bayeux picture of the Hastings castle was excavated at Abinger in Surrey by Brian Hope Taylor in 1949. The mound at Abinger is about thirty metres wide at the base and about twelve metres across the top; it is surrounded by a ditch six metres wide and two and a half metres deep. Hope Taylor uncovered the whole of the top of the mound and he found there a remarkably clear set of post holes. Around the edge was a double line of holes, the outer line set very close together, the inner line more widely spaced. The holes must have contained substantial timbers for they were up to sixty centimetres deep and thirty or more across. These holes indicate that a very formidable stockade had been built around the top of the mound, very much in the same way as is indicated by the scene depicted at Hastings.

Brian Hope Taylor's reconstruction of the structures on the mound at Abinger.

In the centre of the stockade Hope Taylor found a regular arrangement of post holes outlining a square structure three and a half metres across. The holes of this structure were more than a metre deep and it seems likely that it was a good deal taller than the surrounding stockade. Although the picture of the Hastings castle has nothing corresponding to these holes, other castles on the Bayeux Tapestry do. The castle at Dinan in Normandy is shown under attack; the defenders line the stockade on top of the mound, and above their heads projects the superstructure of a tall tower. This is just the sort of structure which could have been built in the centre of the mound at Abinger.

The Abinger castle is a little-known one. It is not mentioned in medieval records and it was probably not in existence for very long; but it is for this reason particularly that it is of such interest. Other castles which were in use for many years were modified and enlarged; they had their timber towers and stockades replaced with stone ones, and their original appearance is now lost. The Abinger castle shows what they must have been like originally, timber and earth structures which could be erected quickly. It is this sort of a castle which William was able to build at Pevensey and Hastings in the sixteen days between his arrival and his battle against Harold.

In one respect the castle at Abinger is not typical, for now there is only a mound and ditch there. Most other castles had an additional enclosure, but if there was one at Abinger it has long since disappeared in the arrangement of the gardens surrounding the mound. The true appearance of an early castle can best be appreciated by looking at the castle at Berkhamsted. William came to Berkhamsted in his march around London after his victory at Hastings and it is probable that the castle was first built there then. Despite the replacement of much that must originally have been in timber by stonework, the earthworks surviving today are probably much as they were first laid out. The castle, like most others, consists of two parts, the mound, known as the motte, with its own defences and surrounding moat, and an extensive open area, known as the bailey, with its own surrounding bank and ditch. The two ditches are linked together and in ideal circumstances were filled with water.

The Normans used the motte and bailey castle to dominate England. The bailey provided sufficient space to house a small garrison which could control the surrounding town or countryside. The motte provided a look-out post and an elevated position from which to fight off attackers, or it could be used as a safe retreat if the bailey should be overrun. Although these castles may not sound very safe places in which to be trapped in a hostile country, they were strong enough to resist the weapons of their day, and events were to prove that they were adequate to suppress Anglo-Saxon opposition to the Norman invaders.

The English had never built castles. There had been no need for them in Saxon England, and when the need came they were not prepared. One Norman writer, Ordericus Vitalis, attributes their defeat entirely to this fact. Though brave and warlike, he says, without castles the English were too weak to resist their enemies. For William, they were the key to his success; everywhere he went he built a castle and when he moved on he left behind him a strongpoint which remained staunchly Norman whatever the loyalties of the surrounding countryside. After the Battle of Hastings he went to Dover; then he approached London in an encircling march which took in Winchester, Wallingford and Berkhamsted. At all these places castles were built. In London he built two castles, one, in the south-east corner of the old Roman city, was the original Tower of London; the other, Baynard's Castle, has now disappeared. William's progress through the country can be mapped by the growing number of castles built by him and then by the Norman nobility.

The attitude of the suppressed Anglo-Saxons may be judged from the findings of recent excavations at Oxford. This castle was built in

A late Saxon house in Oxford! The outline of the house is
indicated by the darker area under the ranging poles in the
centre of the picture. The house was covered by the bank of
the Norman castle, and this in its turn has been cut away in
digging pits, building cellars, and sinking a well. This complicated picture emphasises the difficulty of excavation in
the centre of a town.

1071. It had a motte and bailey; the motte still stands more or less intact as a prominent turf-covered mound overlooking the city. The bailey has long since been built over, though a part of it was uncovered during the construction of new county council offices in 1972 and 1973. This was a typical modern city centre excavation. An enormous hole was dug out for the foundations and basement of the new buildings and the archaeologists had to dig as best they could in the bottom of this hole. The foundation hole had been dug across the eastern edge of the bailey, cutting across the bank and into the ditch. These details were clear enough. The Norman ditch had been dug down through the gravel subsoil into the clay beneath, and a layer of this clay had been plastered against the sloping sides of the ditch to keep the loose gravel in place and to make the ditch watertight.

But, when the material of the Norman bank was removed, underneath it were found layers containing late Saxon objects and features such as rubbish pits and post holes. The rubbish pits contained scraps of pottery and old animal bones, and one even contained a coin—a rare find—a silver halfpenny of King Eadred, 948–952. Nearby were the remains of a late Saxon house. The floor of the house had been dug down into the ground and had fragments of pottery scattered on it. The walls had been built on a framework of solid posts around the edges of the floor. It seems clear that this part of Oxford had been built up and occupied since the tenth century.

All these Saxon features had been covered over by the building of the bank surrounding the Norman bailey. There was absolutely nothing to suggest that the site had been abandoned before the Normans built their castle. Rather, these excavations show that the builders of the Norman castle took little, if any, account of the Saxon houses in the area but swept them all away in the construction of their fortress.

The native reaction can be imagined. The Normans had come as conquerors; they turned people out of their houses and pulled them down to provide a space to build their castles. The resentment amongst the local people must have been very great. No doubt too the Normans added insult to injury by demanding that the Saxons provide the labour to build the castles. It is no wonder if there were outbreaks of rebellion from time to time.

The excavations at Oxford provide an illustration of the way in which the Norman fortifications were imposed on the town. The records in Domesday Book show that the same thing happened elsewhere. At Shrewsbury 51 houses were destroyed to make way for

OPPOSITE
The moat of Oxford Castle, revealed in a builder's trench during the construction of new County Council Offices in 1972. The ladder leans against the black clay lining of the side of the moat.

the castle; at Norwich the number was 113 and at Lincoln as many as 166. Excavations and Domesday Book provide evidence for the Norman fortifications in a number of places; a look at the plans of towns today shows that this was what they did everywhere. Wherever there is a castle in a Saxon town, it is so placed that it must have been

107

built on the site of Saxon houses. The castle at Leicester can serve as an example; it is situated in the south corner of the town, at the important junction of the old Roman wall and the River Soar, and just beside the bridge across the river. From the Norman point of view this was the best position to build, irrespective of what had to be swept away in the process. The position of castles in towns, and the way in which they dominate the townscape, is so striking that even if there was no single surviving document for this period and we had no idea that the Norman Conquest had ever taken place, archaeologists would see the arrival of the 'castle-builders' as the beginning of a new era in England.

The Norman Conquest was totally different from the arrival of the first Anglo-Saxons so many centuries before. The country was not in the state of abandoned chaos which Roman Britain had been; rather it had only recently become unified after centuries of division into small kingdoms. There was not yet, however, a clear line of succession to the throne. Eadwig of Wessex was the first to rule over all England, and he was succeeded by his brother, and then his nephews, Edward the Martyr and Aethelred the Unready. In Aethelred's time England was subject once again to repeated attacks from Denmark, and Swein Forkbeard gained the throne briefly in 1013. When Aethelred died in 1016 the country was divided, its loyalties split between Aethelred's son Edmund Ironside and Swein's son, Cnut of Denmark. Within a year Edmund had died and Cnut was king of England. Cnut was succeeded by his sons, who also ruled in Denmark, but after their deaths the throne returned to Aethelred's son, Edward the Confessor.

Medieval Leicester, showing the position of the castle in relation to the town.

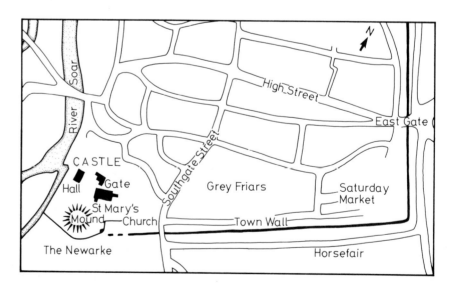

During Cnut's reign Edward had been brought up and educated in Normandy; his inclinations were pro-Norman and it is not surprising that he chose Duke William of Normandy as his heir. Nevertheless when Edward died Harold Godwinson was elected king, for though not of royal blood, his family had been foremost in maintaining order during the internal wars of recent years. But William had not forgotten that he was Edward's choice, and he made his claim to the throne his justification for the Conquest.

However well-meaning his original intentions towards the Anglo-Saxon aristocracy may have been, William soon found that the combined need to remove opposition to himself and to reward his followers resulted in his dispossessing the Anglo-Saxons of their lands and their power, and giving them to his own Normans. Within a very few years of the conquest, the Anglo-Saxon aristocracy was ousted from all positions of real authority, and a new Norman-French ruling class took over. These new rulers made the country what it was to become in the Middle Ages.

BOOKS FOR FURTHER READING

General Works

BLAIR, P. HUNTER An Introduction to Anglo-Saxon England (Cambridge University Press 1956)

PAGE, R. I. Life in Anglo-Saxon England (Batsford 1970)

WHITELOCK, DOROTHY The Beginnings of English Society (Penguin 1952)

WILSON, D. M. The Anglo-Saxons (Thames and Hudson 1960, Penguin 1971)

WILSON, D. M. (ed.) The Archaeology of Anglo-Saxon England (Methuen 1976) contains fully-documented chapters on many of the subjects discussed here.

Special Topics

ALCOCK, LESLIE 'By South Cadbury is that Camelot . . .' (Thames & Hudson 1972)

BROWN, R. A. The Normans and the Norman Conquest (Constable 1969)

BRUCE-MITFORD, R. L. S. The Sutton Hoo Ship Burial (British Museum Handbook, second edition 1972)

CAMERON, KENNETH AND OTHERS Place-Name Evidence for the Anglo-Saxon Invasions and Scandinavian Settlements (English Place-Name Society, School of English, Nottingham University 1975)

TAYLOR, H. M. AND JOAN Anglo-Saxon Architecture (Cambridge University Press 1965)

There are two important annual publications: *Medieval Archaeology* (published by the Society for Medieval Archaeology, Department of Scandinavian Studies, University College, Gower Street, London WC1) includes an annual review of archaeological excavations and other finds of the Anglo-Saxon and Medieval periods. *Anglo-Saxon England* (published by the Cambridge University Press) carries a classified bibliography of all writing, historical, literary and archaeological, on the Anglo-Saxons.

INDEX